THE ROAD FROM SPACE:

How to *find* yourself in the 21st century

SETH MORRIS

http://astro-chologist.com

ISBN: 978-0-9965211-0-9 (Kindle)
ISBN: 978-0-9965211-1-6 (epub)
ISBN: 978-0-9965211-2-3 (softcover)
ISBN: 978-0-9965211-3-0 (hardcover)

Sutekh@astro-chologist.com

Book cover design and layout by, Ellie Bockert Augsburger of CreativeDigital Studios.
www.CreativeDigitalStudios.com

Cover design features:
Vintage Carpenters Square: © RedDaxLuma / Dollar Photo Club
Asphalt Road: © Vitaly Krivosheev / Dollar Photo Club
Classic wind rose isolated on white: © Becker / Dollar Photo Club

Edited by Dustin Schwindt

Formatted by Polgarus Studio

"Millionaires don't use astrology, billionaires do"- J.P. Morgan

Special Thanks

To my family and friends and everyone who has supported me. To my clients and those who have supported me on social media, you are likewise appreciated. I would like to thank the team at Creative Digital Studios for their excellent work. Lastly, would like to that my editor Dustin Schwindt for his hard work.

Contents

Introduction

For many people, life can be a tribulation and, in some cases, seem like punishment. Individuals meander from one thing to the other without ever pinpointing their gifts or perceiving their potential. This is especially true of those in less developed countries who are focused on securing basic necessities. However, even those who have a choice and the opportunity to explore different possibilities, still drift aimlessly despite conveniences.

Imagine a college grad who earns a master's degree in economics but in their 30's decides to switch fields. They may have been pressured into this field by their parents or because they believe it will make them a comfortable living. However, somewhere along the line, they feel something in the pit of their stomach—a burning urge that pulls them in a different direction. In their heart of hearts, they're more of a sensual person, and in their spare time they love cooking. They love working with different flavors and aromas, and they discover that food is something they enjoy so much that they make it their profession and make their way to a successful career as an executive chef. You see? That burning in the pit of your stomach comes from somewhere.

There are ways and methods to speed up this process, ways that will help you determine your hidden talents and passions before you know them. Instead of wondering (and wandering) what you could be doing, wouldn't you like to narrow them down? This can be accomplished using astrology. Yes, astrology.

The astrology I'm speaking of is not the type that you find in the local grocery store checkout line. Predating the 3 Abrahamic religions, astrology is an ancient system of tracking the stars and planets through their orbital transitions and the study of the influence this movement has on us living here on earth. Celestial transitions produce different ranges of magnetic field tonalities that change the nature of our being, and the planets, thought to have different energies that influence living beings, form varying configurations that set the table for specific traits at the biological level. As such, people are born under particular configurations depending on the date, time, and place of their birth. Fundamentally, astrology simply is a system that tracks light cycles and other cycles based on the orbit of the Sun, Moon, and other celestial bodies.

(For each person's time of birth, a unique sky map is drawn called a natal chart. This chart can be accessed using the software links provided in chapter 12.)

Scientists are conflicted on the validity of astrology. Some say that the planets and other celestial bodies have absolutely no impact or effect on living beings on earth. These scientists will cite lack of similarity between the hobbies and careers of identical twins as support. If you observe identical twins, however, you will notice they tend to have the same temperament. Their levels of extraversion or introversion are almost indistinguishable. Other scientists, like Psychiatrist Mitchell E. Gibson have studied and shown a correlation between mental illness potential and *natal charts.* In one case, Brown University's Dr. Chris Ciarleglio studied the light cycle and season of a baby's birth and the effect it had on the child's circadian rhythm and found that there was indeed an effect. This human-celestial cycle relationship is a base tenet of astrology.

For years, I have gotten questions via social media and email regarding specific parts of individuals' natal charts and it is time there was a proper book to answer those questions. There are many astrology books that attempt to explain the reading process of a chart, but they do so in a very *new-agey* way, using terms that are only familiar to those already acquainted with astrology at some level. This book is for the novice. In it, and in the books that follow, I will guide you through each sign and element of the natal chart and introduce you to real world examples and metaphors that anyone can relate to.

This first book is intended as a resource for you to read and understand your own natal chart. You do not need any prior astrological knowledge. Indeed, this book is designed for adults, 18 to 50, who are just getting started, but more specifically for those who have their conscience telling them something in their life is missing. You may be looking for some type of signal or sign, or maybe just an affirmation that you are heading in the right direction. With this book you will be able to pin-point the *what*, *why*, and *how* of your own personal journey.

-1-

The Nucleus (The Sun)

Even if you've never studied astrology, it's likely you've read your horoscope in newspapers and magazines or online. Most likely, it was some overly-vague description of what should take place that day or in the near future. If you're an Aries, it might mention an unknown fortune coming their way, while Virgos might be warned of a tough time at work. These are fun to read, but they're not representative of what astrology is really about. In terms of accuracy or application, these horoscopes are only correct in one sense—the birthdates.

In astrology, we do have a sign, commonly referred to in these horoscopes as the *"Sun sign[1]"*. The Sun sign is the first and arguably most important piece in your *natal chart[2]*. It is based on the 365 day Gregorian solar calendar and the Sun's elliptical course. The angle and placement of the Sun vary month to month, and season to season. These monthly and seasonal changes are the foundation for the astrological concepts of *modalities* and *elements*. I will elaborate on those later. For the time being, we will focus on the Sun.

So what is the Sun sign really?

The Sun is the *engine* of our solar system. The Sun's rays create heat and provide energy to the biosphere so that plants and organisms can grow. The Sun is the earth's engine and makes every system on the planet go. But, astrologically, it does more than that. It reveals our core identity, our

---

[1] The main zodiac sign in one's natal chart, based on the date and time of the solar calendar year.

[2] Personal sky map, snapshot of the cosmic configuration at the time of your birth.

dreams, and what we want to achieve. And, while the exact birthdates make for very nuanced differences from person to person, every astrological month falls into a general Sun sign archetype. In the coming chapters you will learn these archetypes.

Once you get beyond the Sun sign and into the rest of the solar system, you can see this *vehicle* materialize in human form with the Moon showing what kind of interior you have. Do you have a luxury interior? Do you have an athletic interior? Your Moon sign may show a very different style and brand than your engine (*Sun sign*). Each planet after tells us even more. The planet Mercury, for example, shows us how we process and share information. I equate this to the electronics in your vehicle: the tachometer, the cd or mp3 player, or the navigation system.

Each one of these planets mix and match to create a unique human vehicle configured exclusively under the celestial heavens in relation to a particular time and date. Led by the Sun sign, this vehicle is headed toward our astrological destiny.

Unfortunately, many of us end up not listening to or fulfilling that soul urge. Life events pass us by and many times we don't tap into our true potential until later on in life. Tragically, some do not tap into it at all.

Some notes on usage:

- Celestial bodies will always be "in" a certain sign. For example, "the Sun in Aries" means that the Sun from our vantage point is passing through the constellation of Aries. This applies to planets as well. When Venus, for example, passes through the constellation of Aries, we will say Venus is "in" Aries. So the headings in each section will read as (planet) in (zodiac sign).

- In a woman's chart, the Sun and its particular sign and condition shows the characteristics and the type of relationship the woman has with her father. For example, with the Sun in Aries, a woman's father will have the headstrong attitude of a leader, or general. This will have a psychological impact on the daughter.

Your Sun in Aries
March 20ˢᵗ-April 20ᵗʰ

The first step in this journey is to understand the Sun signs and what they really entail. Signs are ordered 1-12 beginning with 3(Aries. Aries begins with the spring equinox, the astrological New Year on March 20th. Aries is also the 1ˢᵗ of the 4 personal signs[3], which represent the beginning of the year or "adolescence ". Aries is exalted as a Sun sign. Exaltation means this placement gives the sign higher than average strength. Strength ratings for each sign can be found in the chart in the *Tables and definitions* chapter of the book.

Aries is a masculine sign[4] and cardinal modality[5] sign belonging to the fire element[6]. What this means is the spirit of the Aries individual is one of a natural starter and leader (whether they get there depends on the rest of the chart). Aries is the pioneer and the warrior. The cardinal modality signifies a burst of energy, direct action, and fire signifies passion. This is how Aries became known as the God of War ruled by the planet Mars. Aries types act spontaneously and inherently want to lead the way. Because they are the fire element, this means their core motivations are not based in sensual desires (earth), logic (air), and empathy (water). They are natural self-starters but aren't that big on persistence of focus (fixed modality) and versatility (mutable modality) unless the rest of their *natal chart* offsets this. That is the beauty of the zodiac: its complementary nature.

Russell Crowe is a good example of an Aries. He played a gladiator in the movies and he has been known off set to be a very fiery and passionate

---

[3] The personal signs are the first 4 signs of the zodiac Aries, Taurus, Gemini, Cancer or the first 3ʳᵈ of the year which represents childhood and personal needs.

[4] Positive element (fire and air) considered the assertive and forward thinking and moving elements.

[5] The energy current of a specific sign. Broken into triplicities representing the beginning, middle, and ending of a season.

[6] One of the 4 temperaments of a specific sign, fire is action oriented and impulsive.

man living up to the lore of his sign. This might explain his bar brawl with rugby players and the fight he started with fellow actor George Clooney. Likewise. Jackie Chan has been an action Kung-Fu star for many decades. An active man in his personal life, he spearheads numerous business endeavors, including a film company and a chain of fitness gyms in China. These personality traits are what makes it easy for these actors to portray action heroes.

Physical Traits:
Aries individuals usually have round and angular heads, ears that lean back and point towards the tips, a prominent nose and cheekbones, a small flat roundish chin, and large eyes. (Note: Physically we show the traits of our Sun, Moon, or Ascendant sign. Sometimes it is only one sign, but usually some mixture of the three.)

Health:
Aries rules the head. Aries may face issues arising from inflammation of the head, for example skin maladies of the scalp, overheating, or stroke. An Aries will often be referred to as a "hot head" ala Russell Crowe, so they should "stay cool" when necessary. Alec Baldwin exhibited this hot head aspect of Aries when left messages on his daughters answering machine screaming enraged and they became public.

Goals:
Aries types enjoy conquest and pioneering. They take the initiative in being a leader and being ahead of the pack. They often become frustrated when goals don't materialize rapidly however. It's important for them to take breaks and relax if they gain too much steam and hit roadblocks.

Famous Sun in Aries people: Russell Crowe, Jackie Chan, Eddie Murphy, Alec Baldwin, Lady Gaga, Robert Downey Jr., Steven Seagal, Pharell Williams, Gary Oldman, Danica Patrick, Big Sean, Payton Manning, Ronaldinho, Anderson Silva.

Sun in Taurus
April 20th –May 20th

Taurus follows next and is a fixed earth sign. This means that Taurus is rooted in the material world and has a slow moving, cautious temperament. Taurus individuals are keen on the 5 senses as the sign's ruler[7] is Venus, the goddess of love and beauty. The aim in the life of most Tauruses is to maintain the status quo. After all, their aim is comfort. As a fixed earth sign, Tauruses are generally averse to acting on impulse (fire), abstracts (air), and emotions (water). Tauruses are also known as foodies and truly enjoy food and drink. They are therefore susceptible to hedonism.

Venus is also the ruler money and possessions, so it's no wonder that Taurus is amongst the top signs represented on the list of the world's billionaires. Money allows the Taurus to buy the comfort they desire. The key to a Taurus finding the right path is decoding the rest of their *natal chart.*

George Clooney is often cast as the cool, charming classic gentleman, which might be art imitating life since he is a Taurus Sun. Megan Fox is often cast as the doe eyed damsel in distress in films. Off screen she is a model published in dozens of magazines.

Physical Traits:
Taurus rules the neck so they have a long or thick neck in most cases. They also possess a squarish head with a strong jaw, cleft chin, and wide-set eyes with thick lids that give off a "sleepy" appearance.

Health:
Taurus rules the neck and throat. Thus maladies relating to the voice, vocal chords, and thyroid are possible.

---

[7] Planet associated with a specific sign.

Goals:

The goals of a Taurus are to gain possessions, increase net-worth, and maintain a life of comfort and pleasure that ensures their personal security and the security of their family. This is where their pride and dignity lies. These individuals can usually excel at real estate related fields, financial planning, and architecture. Since Taurus rules the throat, their claim to fame may be their distinct voice. A Taurus would also likely be a good candidate for the culinary field.

Famous Sun in Taurus people: George Clooney, Michelle Pfeifer, Penelope Cruz, Megan Fox, Malcolm X, Enrique Iglesias, Barbra Streisand, Stevie Wonder, John Cena, George Carlin, Jerry Seinfeld, Ella Fitzgerald.

Sun in Gemini
May 20th- June 22nd

To wrap up the spring season, comes the versatile and communicative Gemini. Since Gemini is an air sign, their *mutable* disposition isn't really one of taking a leadership role and charismatically drawing followers (cardinal) or a pillar of stability (fixed). They don't really express themselves through passion (fire), emotion (water), or practicality (earth) either. These are the communicators, merchants, and public speakers of the zodiac. Often times they are comedians. A Gemini tends to enjoy gossip, the exchange of ideas, and the interpersonal understanding that comes with these exchanges.

A Gemini can relay information through speech very effectively most of the time. But many Geminis also love to text message. A Gemini is also quite capable of being an outstanding communicator through musical mediums, especially hip-hop. Geminis excel in other mediums (such as television) as well.

Marv Albert as the voice of professional basketball is a good example of a Gemini. He has a distinct voice and cadence that is easy to follow. Newt Gingrich, who was speaker of the U.S. House of Representatives is also an impressive orator and public speaker. Amy Schumer, the famous comedian popular for her cutting quick wit is another exemplary Gemini.

Physical Traits:
Geminis tend to have elongated skulls, larger than average jaws and distinct smile lines. They have bright eyes, features that are generally more delicate. Usually look much younger than their age.

Health:
Gemini rules over the nerves, lungs, hands, and shoulders. Because a Gemini has a restless nature and an inclination to pace, this may lead to anxiety and worry, which taxes the nervous system. Methods that help a Gemini to focus, such as meditation, will go a long way.

Goals:
To be heard and speak their mind and exchange ideas. Human interaction is important and learning through human interaction. This is where their pride lies. Geminis should look into communications as a possible career.

Famous Sun in Gemini people: Johnny Depp, Angelina Jolie, Paul McCartney, Tupac Shakur, Kanye West, Prince, Amy Schumer, John Fitzgerald Kennedy, Newt Gingrich, Marv Albert, Mike Breen, Mark Wahlberg, Dean Martin, Miles Davis, Morgan Freeman, George H.W. Bush, Lauryn Hill, Heidi Klum.

Sun in Cancer
June 22nd- July 22nd

With Cancer, we arrive back at the cardinal modality. Cancer is the beginning of the summer and begins on the summer solstice. We therefore come back to the cardinal self-starter or initiating energy, but this time it's in an emotional and sensitive water sign. Logic (air), pragmatism (earth), and faith (fire) are not a part of the core spirit in the Cancer individual.

Their goal is to protect their home and their family. In that sense, a Cancer is like a defense-first-oriented Mars sign.

Cancers are emotionally engaged with whatever they may be pursuing and will cling to it even if its time has passed. But above all, Cancer individuals take pride in caring for others. The Moon, which rules Cancer, represents the archetypal mother energy. So Cancers are often content with tending to their home and taking care of their family, and Cancer men are especially dedicated to their mothers. Cancers take pride in staying true to their past.

Robin Williams, Kevin Hart, and Will Ferrell express the emotions of a Cancer through their zany form of slapstick comedy. In their personal lives family is something they all talk about extensively in interviews, especially their kids in true Cancer fashion.

Physical Traits:
Cancers have round faces and heads in most cases. They also may have pointed chins, a short nose bone, wide forehead, larger or smaller than average eyes, and they often gain weight around the stomach.

Health:
Cancer corresponds to the Stomach; therefore, proper digestion is important to a Cancer as is taking time to relax while eating. Their stomach is sensitive to extremes of the 4 flavors of cooking which are; sweet, sour, salty, and bitter. Too much cold food may produce mucus and cause colds. Cancers should also watch how much alcohol they consume. (Cancer's confidence can waiver and they may become reliant on the uninhibited effects alcohol offers.)

Goals:
Cancers desire to provide care, nourishment, and hospitality to others. It is important as a water sign for Cancers to work in an inviting and familiar environment. Like Taurus, Cancer is likely to do well in the hospitality industry.

Famous Sun in Cancer people: Tom Cruise, Tom Hanks, Harrison Ford, Meryl Streep, Ariana Grande, Will Ferrell, Sofia Vergara, Bill Cosby, O.J. Simpson, Derek Jeter, Mel Brooks, Lionel Messi, Prince William, Robin Williams, Princess Diana, George W. Bush, Kevin Hart.

Sun in Leo
July 23rd- August 21st

The first four signs (personal signs) tend to have more personal goals. As we enter the middle of summer the Sun enters Leo. Leo is the Sun's domicile[8] sign and its strongest position. Think of the power and quality of the Sun in late July and early August in the Northern hemisphere. The Sun is hot and bright and contains the source of all life.

Leo is a fixed fire sign, so the best way to picture Leo is as a king or queen on their throne. They bask in the glory and dignity of their position as ruler. They rule with courage, pride, and a benevolent disposition; however, they don't want to forfeit their position, nor want new advisors (Leos have an aversion to cardinal and mutable modalities). Leos are not necessarily empathetic (water) or logic ruled (air), and they prefer not to be simply a manager of bureaucracy (earth). They want to achieve accolades and earn respect even if it's not the center stage grandeur that is attributed to them in the cookie-cutter horoscopes of magazines.

Barack Obama and Bill Clinton make the Sun in Leo list. Many other heads of state are Leos, such as former Venezualan president Hugo Chavez. Leos love the prestige associated with those leadership positions.

This love of adulation also leads many Leos into show business. Halle Berry, a Leo, is an actress and model most well known for her style and attractiveness. Jennifer Lopez similarly is a singer and actress known for her style as well. Magic Johnson who was the leader and catalyst for the

---

[8] A planet's home sign, and where it is most powerfully expressed. Think of a football team with home field advantage, in a weather that's the norm for that city.

"showtime" Lakers is a Leo, who brought flash and style to his sport.

Arnold Schwarzenegger as a major action star as well as California's former governor has thrived in the Hollywood limelight and as a leader. With his physique he also epitomizes a third quality of the Leo as Leos (along with Libras) are drawn to bodybuilding.

Physical Traits:
Leos have prominent noses, and, like Taurus, they tend to have squarish/round heads. Leos also have pointy chins that are sometimes cleft. Their skin also may have an orange hue regardless of race.

Health:
Leo rules the heart. As such, Leo rules heart conditions, such as heart attacks and strokes. Leos should make a point of eating tomatoes as studies have shown that the lycopene in Tomatoes lowers the risk of coronary heart disease (The tomato actually contains 4 chambers like the heart).

Goals:
Leos long to be noticed and acknowledged, most of all respected. They want to impress others. However, Leos must remember they are not entitled to anything just because of their ego. They must work for it. When they create or accomplish something of note, and receive all due praise for it, they are at their best. Being able to take pride in their name, identity, and legacy.

Famous Sun in Leo people: Barack Obama, Ben Affleck, Madonna, Jennifer Lopez, Carl Jung, Arnold Schwarzenegger, Whitney Houston, Halle Berry, Bill Clinton, Hugo Chavez, Usain Bolt, Kylie Jenner, Magic Johnson, Henry Ford, Triple H, Martin Sheen, Aldous Huxley.

Sun in Virgo
August 22nd-September 23rd

At the end of summer comes the mutable earth sign of Virgo. Virgo is humble (earth), grounded, versatile (mutable) and is known as the nurse sign. Virgo is one of the healing signs along with Scorpio and Pisces. But Virgo is a practical caretaker. Mercury provides Virgo with the ability to spot small discrepancies and fix them, perfect them, and then move on.

An emergency room nurse who has to look over notes and deal with dozens of patients is likely a Virgo or has prominent Virgo energy in their chart. Virgos are hands on, and have a changeable energy. They want to operate in a clean and orderly environment. This is also the sign of the mechanic because they have the ability to see how individual components work within a machine. Virgos want their day to day routine to flow efficiently and without hitches.

Musicians and entertainers such as Amy Winehouse and Michael Jackson went for such perfection in their music and performances. Michael Jackson was a notorious workhorse. One of Jackson's acquaintances is quoted on the subject: "Michael's a machine, Michael was insane, Michael was obsessed with perfection." Similarly, George R.R. Martin is famous for the long and very detail oriented *A Song of Ice and Fire* (aka *Game of Thrones*) fantasy book series.

Physical Traits:
Virgo women tend to have large and "innocent" bright eyes. Virgos have distinct smile lines and have a cleft chin and nose in many cases.

Health:
Virgo rules the digestive system, particularly the abdomen and bowels. Virgo is ruled by Mercury, so they are prone to nervous disorders, especially nervous disorders associated with the digestive system. Virgos thus should pay attention to their health and hygiene and eat easily digestible meals.

Goals:

Service and healing come naturally to Virgos. Analytical and mechanical work are fields where Virgos can also excel. Lastly, communications and writing are very Virgo-oriented fields because of the requisite attention to detail. Virgos should be aware of their perfectionism. It is important to perfect one's work, but it is important to finish work and move on to the next task, rather than wait for the *perfect* time and become idle.

Famous Sun in Virgo people: Amy Winehouse, Hugh Grant, Freddie Mercury, Sean Connery, Nas, Michael Jackson, Beyonce Knowles, Kobe Bryant, Jimmy Fallon, Ray Charles, Billy Ray Cyrus, Louis C.K., Bill O'Reilly, Moby, Phil Jackson, Sanaa Lathan, George R.R. Martin.

Sun in Libra
September 23rd-October 22nd

Following the summer comes the fall equinox and the cardinal air sign of Libra. Libras are logic-oriented (air) as opposed to emotional (water), passionate (fire), or practical (earth). Libra rules over the arts and the skill of debate. Therefore, Libras are talented at deal making, art, music, and objective judgement of two opposing sides.

In a management setting, Libras will delegate in a manner they see as fair and use suggestion by laying out pros and cons of an argument. They attempt to bring two opposing sides together when faced with a conflict. If they sense inequality, they may initiate an argument or debate in order to reach a just conclusion. Libras have a friendly, sanguine temperament. In astrological terms, Libra is considered in "fall[9]" as their personal desires take a back seat to what they see as the objective truth, which may in some cases favor someone else. They take great pride in their relationships and partnerships which form their identity.

Rapper Snoop Dogg is known for his ladies' man pimp persona and

---

[9] In a weakened state, not operating at full power.

music which is perfect for Venus. Libras use the powers of persuasion and attraction and are often known to have silver tongues. Judge Judy is famous for her TV small claims court show where she is cutting and tough, but fair minded. As a Libra, she discerns lies from falsehoods with logic and reasoning.

Physical Traits:
Libras tend to have a small receding chin (sometimes cleft) and bright, heavy-lidded eyes. They gain weight around the midsection and usually have some form of swayback (Lordosis). Libras also have a round bulbous cranium. High, round cheekbones

Health:
Libra rules the kidneys and buttocks. They may suffer Illness of the urinary tract, poor assimilation of fluids (watch alcohol intake), lower back weakness and swayback. According to TCM practitioners, the Goji berry (or Wolfberry) has a positive effect on the kidneys and Liver.

Goals:
Libras seek to merge two sides in a collaborative fashion and to bring about peaceful resolutions in tense situations. They show creativity in art and music and excel as lawyers, judges, and deal brokers. Libras tend to have looking-glass selves, so it is important for them to cultivate their own unique identities. Any field that engages them creatively such as music, or takes advantage of their charm and looks would be prosperous for them.

Famous Sun in Libra: Will Smith, Zac Efron, Matt Damon, Monica Bellucci, Usher, Snoop Dogg, Hugh Jackman, T.I., Deepak Chopra, Mahatma Gandhi, Chuck Berry, Lil Wayne, Jim Henson, Jimmy Carter, Jeff Goldblum, Christopher Reeve, Amber Rose, Judge Judy.

Sun in Scorpio
October 22nd- November 22nd

Scorpio follows Libra and brings in the middle of autumn. Scorpio is a fixed water sign which is emotionally driven and draws on ample stores of willpower in order to attack goals. Scorpios generally want to achieve positions of power but prefer to remain behind the scenes to exercise that power. Scorpios are averse to change, but they shine through being perceptive and intuitive to drive them to where they want to go. Scorpios take pride in their psychological abilities and willpower.

Whatever a Scorpio does, there will be a psychological component to how they maneuver about the world. Scorpios hide their identity until they trust someone. Scorpios have a phlegmatic temperament. As a water sign ruled by Mars, they use toughness and a cold exterior as a form of protection, sometimes employing misdirection to throw off people they don't trust.

Leonardo DiCaprio, a Scorpio, is known for the intensity he brings to his wide variety of characters he plays on screen. These characters usually have some deep psychological quirks and are eccentric. His portrayal of Wall Street conman Jordan Belfort in *The Wolf of Wall Street* and Howard Hughes in *The Aviator* demonstrate the intensity a Scorpio actor is capable of. Joaquin Phoenix brings similar intensity to his quirky characters. Hillary Clinton is a Scorpio who has displayed a consistent toughness in her public life. She is an intense polarizing figure, often considered cold by those who do not know her. This type of criticism is common for a Scorpio.

Physical Traits:
Scorpios tend to have larger than average features, especially eyes, which also tend to be light hues in many cases.

Health:
Scorpio rules the sexual reproductive organs and elimination organs; therefore, Scorpio is associated with troubles in the urinary tract, colon,

vaginal canal and urethra. These organs and systems should be maintained carefully. It is important for Scorpios, like Cancer to watch alcohol and drug intake.

Goals:

Scorpios strive to discover and uncover hidden truths. They want to be self-sufficient and independent of others, gaining power and control, even if it is just power or merely control of their own life. That's where their pride lies. Scorpios also are likely go through a few earth shattering transformational life experiences in their lives.

Famous Sun in Scorpio people: Joaquin Phoenix, Anne Hathaway, Hillary Clinton, Bjork, Leonardo DiCaprio, Grace Kelly, Kris Jenner, Bruce Jenner, Charles Bronson, Oscar Pistorious, Aaron Hernandez, Bill Gates, Katy Perry, Julia Roberts.

Sun in Sagittarius
November 22nd-December 22nd

Sagittarius is the final fire sign in the astrological year and a mutable fire sign that ends the fall season. Mutability (versatile, erratic) and Fire (passionate, spirited) makes Sagittarius a versatile and energetic spirit. As such, the Sagittarius will be focused on a number of tasks at any given time. They are a "Jack of all trades." Faith driven (fire) as opposed to logical (air) emotional (water), or practical (earth), a Sagittarius wants to understand the reason why things exist as they do. Sagittarius pride lies in their intellect.

Sagittarians are explorers in many contexts and generally inquisitive people. Sagittarius rules foreign travel and International/intercultural relations. You might see a Sagittarius as a travel agent, tour guide, or other travel related job.

Sagittarius also rules comedy and Sagittarians fit well into the role of jester. There is a long list of Sagittarius comedians.

John Kerry uses his Sagittarius temperament in his current role as

Secretary of State of the United States, travelling around the world engrossed in different cultures as a diplomat. Sagittarians Jamie Foxx, Redd Foxx, and Jon Stewart are also well known comedians and entertainers.

Physical Traits:
Sagittarians usually have elongated heads with high foreheads. Sagittarius rules the thighs and hips, so these areas tend to be noticeably more prominent especially on women.

Health:
Sagittarius rules the hips and sciatic nerve, so nerve problems with the legs, especially in the hips, are associated with Sagittarius. Sagittarians are also prone to accidents because of their haphazard way of going about things.

Goals:
Sagittarians try to explore and learn from new experiences and share these experiences with others. They enjoy life and want to have fun. A career with a lot of change suits Sagittarians. They would excel as a traveling lecturer or a travel agent, something that, while challenging, allows for freedom and versatility.

Famous Sun in Sagittarius people: Brad Pitt, Taylor Swift, Scarlett Johansson, Samuel L. Jackson, Jay-Z, Jimi Hendrix, Tina Turner, Nicki Minaj, Joseph Stalin, Rita Ora, Jeff Bridges, Dwight Howard, Jamie Foxx, Redd Foxx, Julianne Moore, Woody Allen, Steven Spielberg, John Kerry, Jon Stewart.

Sun in Capricorn
December 22nd-January 20th

Capricorn is the first sign of the winter season. Once again, since this is a sign that begins a season, it's a cardinal sign (a manager or leader) and belongs to the earth element (practical, tactile). This is the business person and boss of the zodiac. Ruled by Saturn, there is a more subdued and melancholic temperament with these individuals and a tendency to suffer from depression and Seasonal Affective Disorder (SAD). While Sagittarians are known for their grin, Capricorns are known for their poker face. Capricorns appreciate order and work to achieve goals by systematically laying out long term plans and working persistently to reach those goals. Capricorns take pride in their careers and work.

Denzel Washington and Bradley Cooper are two famous Capricorn actors working today. Denzel Washington is known for his stoic and calculating characters such as detective Alonzo Harris in *Training* Day. Off-screen he is also a serious person who takes his craft seriously. Actress Betty White has had a career in entertainment for over 70 years, beginning with radio in 1939, and she's known for her straight-faced comedy and dry wit.

Physical Traits:
Capricorns tend to have a stoic look about them. They possess a straight brow line and symmetrical features.

Health:
Capricorn rules the knees, so the knees need special care in many cases. Circulation is an issue with Capricorns, so warm foods that promote circulation will help them. Due to the lack of circulation they tend to catch colds. Being too rigid may result in physical stiffness.

Goals:
Capricorns strive to climb the career ladder and become established as an authority in their respective field. They want to gain material security from their career and work consistently and often. It is important for them to step out of the box every once in a while and approach life in a spontaneous way.

Famous Sun in Capricorn people: Mel Gibson, Bradley Cooper, Nicolas Cage, Sade Adu, Al Capone, Humphrey Bogart, Rod Stewart, Ted Cruz, R.Kelly, Dwyane Wade, Katie Couric, Denzel Washington, David Bowie, Elvis Presley, Catherine Duchess of Cambridge, Betty White.

Sun in Aquarius
January 20th-February 20th

Aquarius is a fixed air sign that lies in the Sun's detriment because mid-winter is when the Sun is at its lowest power. Contrary to Leo's cheerful and charismatic outlook, Aquarius is very restrained and controlled thanks to its ruler Saturn. Many mistake Aquarius for a water sign because of its symbol, the water bearer, but Aquarius is indeed an air sign. Aquarius is a fixed (midseason) mid-winter air sign that's stable, even-keeled, and logical.

Aquarians have a sanguine temperament, so their energy is *light* and friendly. Fields that involve electronics are usually their strong suit, and they excel at sciences in general. Aquarians are also humanitarian minded and able to see how large groups like non-profits should operate. With their big picture conscious mind they can see what particular skillset a person has and where they fit in an organization. Aquarius takes pride in being different. However in a detached cerebral way that can be perceived as cold and apathetic to some. This pride in being different often means that they are comfortable with being loners.

Many famous Aquarians bring about collective change and innovation in their own rights. Bob Marley, through his music, influenced change in societal racial oppression and injustice. His influence spread worldwide changing the consciousness of humans of every race and creed. Oprah Winfrey through media enterprise has changed the media landscape for women and black women specifically. Beginning as a local news reporter she now runs the Oprah Winfrey Network (OWN). These two are trailblazers in their own way.

Physical Traits:

Aquarians are ruled by the ankles, so their ankles usually appear larger or more developed than average. They have bright and alert eyes, often light-hued. Aquarius is a Saturn sign that signifies the depth of winter so their skin may be more pale and veiny than average.

Health:

Aquarius rules the ankles, so Aquarians are likely to have strong and visibly large calf muscles. As the opposite of Leo and being in detriment there is a tendency to suffer from weakened heart strength.

Goals:

Aquarians attempt to bring about innovation through scientific innovation. Aquarians also work to create social change through collective ideals. Aquarians tend to be friendly but loners, so they should be given space. The I.T. field is something that should interest many Aquarians.

Famous Sun in Aquarius people: John Travolta, Ellen DeGeneres, Alicia Keys, Oprah Winfrey, Jennifer Aniston, Michael Jordan, Hakeem Olajuwon, Bob Marley, Sarah Palin, Paul Ryan, Chris Rock, Dr. Dre, Ayn Rand, Kerry Washington, Eckhart Tolle.

Sun in Pisces
February 20th – March 20th

Pisces ends the zodiac. Pisces is a mutable water sign indicating its nature as vacillating, emotional and intuitive. Pisces is the opposite of Virgo, but like Virgo is a caretaker by nature. While Virgo takes care of the seen, Pisces takes care of the unseen and voiceless, the drug addict or the prisoner for example. Pisces strive to achieve the higher ideals of Jupiter through spirituality and non-judgmental caretaking. Pisces take pride in their ability to sacrifice and serve others. Pisces also take pride in their spiritual abilities.

Because Pisces is so intuitive and tapped into the universal psyche, they are often gifted at channeling many emotions through art, whether it be visual arts like painting, film, and photography or other forms such as music and poetry. Like their Jupiter cousin Sagittarius, there is also a comedic ability many times here.

Kurt Cobain was an extremely emotional Pisces, so engrossed in music that substance abuse became an outlet for his self-destructive. Pisces rules such self-destruction. Erykah Badu is a musician, and poet. She is also a midwife/doula that helps deliver babies through natural birthing techniques.

Physical Traits:

Pisces eyes seem to be either very large or very small. The individuals with larger eyes show the whites of their eyes like the fish that Pisces represents. Pisces have short noses, wide mouths, and exaggerated jawlines.

Health:

Pisces rules over the feet and the lymphatic system. They are susceptible to blood borne illnesses and gout. It's important for them to consume water and get cardiovascular exercise.

Goals:

Pisces often assist others in their healing process. They try to create other worldly music and art and photography. They make good spiritual guides and motivators, but they should Identity and clearly define their boundaries. Careers related to religion and healthcare are best suited for them.

Famous Sun in Pisces people: Rihanna, Kurt Cobain, Justin Bieber, Tony Robbins, Floyd Mayweather Jr., Seal, Erykah Badu, Nina Simone, Terrence Howard, Rob Lowe, Ted Kennedy, Chelsea Clinton, Shaquille O'Neal, Ellen Page, Chuck Norris.

Conclusion on Sun Signs

These energies represent the core identities of individuals. In your *natal chart,* there are other planets that affect the rest of your identity. If the Sun is the engine of the vehicle, the other 9 planets are the rest of the car and are also required to make it operate. What good is an engine with no wheels? Or no seats? The planets and the specific season they were in at the time of your birth represent integral parts of you as a person.

There are 6 planets in traditional astrology and 9 in modern astrology. I will focus on the traditional astrological planets in this book. These 6 planets have a much longer history dating back thousands of years and have been practiced with integrity ever since. The modern planets (Uranus, Neptune, and Pluto) did not have a sign rulership and have only been used for a few hundred years. (Uranus was the first to be "discovered" and introduced in 1781.)

-2-
The Home (The Moon)

Domicile means home. In astrology, the Moon is the indicator of your internal climate, the way you respond to outside stimuli, and your comfort zone. This is the 2nd luminary[10] in your *natal chart* and just as important as your Sun sign. Your Moon sign is the 2nd piece in the puzzle that is your *natal chart*. In some schools of astrology, your Moon sign is actually more important than your Sun sign. Here, though, we are staying with the western/*tropical* zodiac.

In many ancient polytheistic cultures around the world, the Moon has a goddess of some sort as its deity. Symbolically, the Moon represents our mother and our relationship with her. The Moon sign in a man's chart shows what kind of woman he is attracted to as a wife, and also shows his relationship with his own mother. In a woman's chart, her Moon is drawn to a man's Sun but in a more subtle way.

Moon shows man's ideal wife

These characteristics show the nature of the woman a man is most likely to settle down with and marry.

Your Moon in Aries

Moon in Aries is a cardinal fire sign. The Moon in Aries gives the native

---

[10] The Sun and Moon in your natal chart, rule the night and day cycle.

quick fight and flight impulses in response to a situation. As a personal sign and the first sign, Aries can be quick to anger for reasons that may seem childish especially to lunar earth and air signs, who are more cautious and thoughtful by nature. If bored, an Aries Moon will say so, as they want to constantly move forward. The Aries Moon is often thinking "me first" and "I want it my way" when approaching a situation.

Moon in Aries is most comfortable when things are going their way, especially in an activity like a recreational sport. Losing negatively affects the Aries Moon's mood. When the Aries Moon native gets angry in an argument they are losing, you may see the horns of the ram pop out and they begin to get louder and more aggressive as opposed to using reason. The anger here isn't calculated or malicious really; it's just on a short fuse. When all is said and done, this is a position of someone quick to act in response to a situation, and if this energy is deprived of release, it will affect the native's health negatively. The native wants a partner who is a go getter. The native's impulse will be to spring into action as opposed to deliberate.

What this means for the Moon in Aries individual:
There is a rush to anger with this placement, which may lead to confrontations, but there is a great youthful spirit inside. The Moon in Aries native responds very quickly to challenges in a passionate and emotional way.

The Moon in Aries Comfort Zone:
Aries Moons want to be in charge, have their way, and want instant gratification in most cases. Being independent emotionally and otherwise is important to them. They are uncomfortable with hyper-sensitive and overly rigid individuals.

Famous Moon in Aries people: Rihanna, T.I., Chuck Norris, Nas, Bill Gates, Steve Jobs, Angelina Jolie, Lebron James, Sade Adu, Chris Rock, Amber Rose, Cillian Murphy, Louis Armstrong, Joe Pesci, The Game.

Moon in Taurus

Following headstrong Aries, comes the fixed earth sign Taurus. The Moon is exalted[11] in Taurus and comfortable there because Taurus is a Venus sign and rules money, possessions, and sensual comforts. As a fixed sign, this is a stable Moon. Moon in Taurus individuals want to be surrounded by a comfortable environment, wear comfortable clothes, and enjoy quality food and drink. Sensual pleasures are nourishment for these people.

Don't force Moon in Taurus to change their routines and rituals because it will be met with resistance. They can be very stubborn but are also committed. They can be possessive if their stability is threatened by someone else, particularly a significant other. Moon in Taurus likes to "own" things, including people. The Moon in Taurus native is cool and calm until there is something that is really bothering them or upsetting their routine.

What this means for the Moon in Taurus individual:
They are adverse to change or risk, but don't allow stagnation to hinder personal progress due to comfort and owning a lot of possessions.

The Moon in Taurus Comfort Zone:
Maintaining material possessions and a secure, comfortable home and being financially secure are important to Moon in Taurus's piece of mind. They may have intimacy trouble with flamboyant and prideful personalities who like to impress. also with *heady* types who neglect physical and material needs.

Famous Moon in Taurus people: Rafael Nadal, Bill Clinton, Robert Downey Jr., Bob Dylan, Chris Brown, Prince Harry of Wales, Pharell Williams, Quintin Tarantino, Kobe Bryant, Ronald Reagan, William Shatner, Dennis Rodman, Keyshia Cole.

---

[11] Not as strong as domicile or home sign (I.e. Sun in Leo, or Moon in Cancer). Favored position.

Moon in Gemini

When the Moon enters Gemini, it goes through a wide array of "emotions" due to the vacillating nature of Mercury. When upset, this placement is more likely to express anger verbally as opposed to emotions or brooding. Moon in Gemini wants to talk their feelings out. As a personal sign, Moon in Gemini will speak from a personal perspective, but they are not necessarily concerned about what the listener thinks, or even if they're really listening at all. This native is at their most comfortable when there is an audience for their thoughts.

A Gemini wants listeners, an audience. This is the sign of the orator. Since the Moon is the unconscious mind, the need to speak isn't really active; instead, it is something that just happens. Moon in Gemini are susceptible to respiratory illnesses due to stress and burnout.

What this means for the Moon in Gemini individual:
They like to chat and express themselves emotionally through words. They are encouraged to slow down and sometimes practice silence. Silent reflection is of great help to the Moon in Gemini native.

The Moon in Gemini Comfort Zone:
Moon in Gemini enjoys open lines of communication, speaking their mind and having someone to listen to them. Being able to communicate as a way to decompress is important to them. Intimacy with people who don't seem mentally engaged, such as dreamy types, may be disconcerting. They feel the need to be rubbing elbows with others.

Famous Moon in Gemini people: Barack Obama, Vladimir Putin, 50 cent, Jim Carrey, Jeff Bridges, Jeremy Renner, Kirk Douglas, Bernard Hopkins, John McEnroe, John Goodman, Kristen Wiig, David Rockerfeller, Krs-One, Jennifer Lawrence.

Moon in Cancer

Moon in Cancer is at home there. This indicates that the native has a strong emotional nature that feels most comfortable with familiar surroundings and familiar people. So Moon in Cancer can be extremely attached to family and home. There is a keen sense of other people's moods and needs. Cancer is the archetypal "mother" sign after all. As a personal sign, the emotions are most influenced when something affects them personally or affects someone close to them. There isn't necessarily huge empathy or concern for an abstract "mass" of people such as with Pisces.

Cancer is a starch and sugar lover, so, much like Moon in Taurus, Moon in Cancer will indulge themselves, sometimes too much. Because of this, they may gain weight around the mid-section. Moon in Cancer can be cagey and reserved mostly as a defense mechanism. They can also take things too personally. However, these traits may change with time and experience.

What this means for the Moon in Cancer individual:
Moon in Cancer natives are encouraged to get out of their comfort zone. Not everything said should be taken personally. Also, they should understand that past situations and their outcomes do not indicate how a new situation will play out.

The Moon in Cancer Comfort Zone:
A safe and stable home environment with money in the bank is important for their wellbeing. A healthy relationship with their mother and their family is very important. Intimacy may be a problem with those who are very independent and aggressive, and also very cool, flirty, and detached.

Famous Moon in Cancer people: Jimi Hendrix, Colin Ferrell, Sofia Vergara, Taylor Swift, Kurt Cobain, Shakira, Keanu Reeves, Sean Penn, Harrison Ford, Drake, Mos Def, Kris Jenner, Lisa Lopes, Mark Ruffalo, Clark Gable, Prince William Duke of Cambridge, Catherine Duchess of Cambridge.

Moon in Leo

The Moon in Leo native wants to be recognized and acknowledged most of all. Doing something of note and receiving the due accolades makes them feel whole. The Sun rules Leo, so this is a more ego-centered Moon than the other two fire signs. As a fixed sign, they are more stable and seek stability by being the center or foundation and having others revolve around them (like the planets around the Sun). Also as a fixed sign, loyalty is very important and such loyalty will be returned.

If embarrassed, the lunar Leo may take an especially long time to lick its wounds and recover. They like to impress others so don't show them up. Moon in Leo is slower to anger than Aries, and more stable than Sagittarius. Let them shine. They will do so more quietly than the Leo Sun native. The men with this placement seek a spouse they can be proud of, someone who is playful and that they can show off.

<u>What this means for the Moon in Leo individual:</u>
They should take pride in all that they do. They won't impress everyone but that's ok. They should also remember that the world doesn't revolve around them.

<u>The Moon in Leo Comfort Zone:</u>
Moon in Leo enjoys being respected and acknowledged. They like to impress others and have a strong subconscious yearning for the acknowledgement associated with impressing others. They may have intimacy issues with possessive and secretive emotional types, also with very materialistic people.

Famous Moon in Leo people: Tom Cruise, Katie Holmes, Tom Hanks, Bruno Mars, Clint Eastwood, Megan Fox, Julia Roberts, David Bowie, Paris Hilton, Sean Bean, Carlos Santana, Mark Hamill.

Moon in Virgo

Moon in Virgo is constantly thinking and analyzing. As a mutable sign, it's a highly changeable placement. The native is emotionally compelled through working and helping others. They do this not necessarily in an empathetic way (Earth element), but in a practical way, through service. Moon in Virgo does not emote in the water sign sense but talks their emotions out or expends a kind of energy by cleaning or working.

Moon in Virgo can suffer from digestive issues because of the amount of occurrences that get on their "nerves". They may be very picky about their food intake; however, this doesn't necessarily mean they will choose healthy foods. This native will analyze their feelings, obsess, and fuss especially when they don't believe they're being as perfect as they believe they're capable. This results in them being very self-critical. They can worry themselves into inaction.

What this means for the Moon in Virgo Individual:
Being a workaholic and in constant worry can be very taxing. It's important to that they periodically just let things play out as they may. They have the knack for writing

The Moon in Virgo Comfort Zone:
They feel at ease caring for others through service, enjoying work and being busy. When they are upset or annoyed harsh criticism flows from anger. Their homes tend to be very sanitary even if it is messy. Not comfortable with emotionalism. Intimacy with very talkative people who aren't focused on action or highly enthusiastic carefree people can be an issue.

Famous Moon in Virgo people: Madonna, John Fitzgerald Kennedy, Nicki Minaj, Zac Efron, John Travolta, Samuel L Jackson, DMX, Blake Lively, Bill Cosby, Hulk Hogan, Sean Combs, CM Punk, Ted Kennedy, Deepak Chopra, Serena Williams, Jack Nicholson, Natalie Portman.

Moon in Libra

Moon in Libra is a more tempered placement for the Moon as Venus rules Libra. Moon in Libra wants to relate on a one on one basis and is comfortable in small groups and being part of a pair. Being alone may actually make this native uncomfortable or ill at ease. On a deep emotional level, Moon in Libra is not, however, consistent with traditional lunar characteristics. It's an intellectual, social way of relating. Water Moon signs may see it as a *superficial* way of relating. The Moon in Libra is prone to start debates and to argue when argument is not really called for. Libra is a Cardinal air sign, so, at its core, Libra wants to move forward; therefore, when bored, an argument or *debate* may be started.

What this means for the Moon in Libra Individual:
Partnership and making connections is wonderful for the Moon in Libra native. However, Moon in Libra is encouraged to take the lead and not leave decisions up to others.

The Moon in Libra Comfort Zone:
Moon in Libra desires a peaceful environment with no conflicts. They prefer being in the company of another person. It is important to become comfortable with some independence. Intimacy with someone who is very formal and emotionally reserved, and someone who is very sensitive and emotional can be a challenge.

Famous Moon in Libra people: Mel Gibson, Jay-z, Leonardo DiCaprio, Alicia Keys, Bradley Cooper, Steven Seagal, Fergie, Kate Winslet, Edward Norton, Ariana Grande, Joseph Stalin, Justin Bieber, Grace Jones, Shemar Moore.

Moon in Scorpio

Since it's a Mars sign, Moon in Scorpio is in the Moon's fall[12]. The Moon indicates self-care and a Scorpio Moon has a conqueror's energy. To feed themselves, Moon in Scorpio natives tend to siphon from others whether it be emotionally or financially. This is until they build their own nest and feel secure.

Moon in Scorpio is more emotionally stable than the other water signs because it's a fixed sign. However, these natives can lose it and explode after working hard to stay calm and keep emotions in check. Scorpio moons are fed through sexual fulfillment and control. There is a need to control environments and keep tabs on what is going on around them. If things aren't accounted for, this is when Moon in Scorpio may become uneasy and more alert. Cutting sarcasm or spitefulness will result if they are hurt or their security is threatened. Moon in Scorpio natives can be affectionate, but they are selective. They do not want to be seen as vulnerable which may seem like a weakness to them. They are also good at keeping a poker face.

What this means for the Moon in Scorpio individual:
They appreciate intensity and have a deep emotional reservoir, so It's important that they not use their keen senses to manipulate others.

The Moon in Scorpio Comfort Zone:
Moon in Scorpio natives prefer being in control and enjoy emotional intimacy and closeness. They need privacy and a secure place to recharge. Moon in Scorpios have intimacy trouble with people who are too cerebral and detached emotionally, as well as showoffs.

Famous Moon in Scorpio people: Jennifer Lopez, Beyonce Knowles, Scarlett Johansson, Mariah Carey, Bruce Lee, Bob Marley, Elizabeth Taylor, Will Smith, Bono, Mitt Romney, Mila Kunis, Meagan Good, Snoop Dogg, Mark Zuckerberg.

---

[12] Fall is a place of lower power for that particular planet. Stronger than detriment however.

Moon in Sagittarius

The Moon in Sagittarius native is going to be most at home in foreign surroundings and around different types of people. They may feel most at home after they leave their parent's home or after they move to a foreign country with a new culture to learn about and explore. Their spouse may be of a completely different race, religion, or ethnicity. Moon in Sagittarius needs the freedom to explore these options. This is the healthy curiosity that feeds them. If that passion is stifled and their curiosity hindered, they become dissatisfied emotionally.

As a mutable sign, this Moon has an especially hard time with boredom since Sagittarius' nature is to explore and learn. Questioning their judgement or criticizing their beliefs or intellect will hurt them more so than a personal attack. The Moon in Sagittarius native wants a partner who is interesting, someone they can learn from, who is fun to be around and supports their curiosity of things unknown.

<u>What this means for the Moon in Sagittarius native:</u>
When someone challenges their intellect, they are offended. It's important for the Moon in Sagittarius native to remain consistent and not to blow off obligations or wait until the last minute.

<u>The Moon in Sagittarius Comfort Zone:</u>
Moon in Sagittarius individuals feel comfortable in a foreign country, an upbeat and positive environment or in a large residence. There is a yearning in this individual to move their residence often. They like to move often and enjoy experiences with a philosophical meaning. Intimacy with individuals who are very critical and reductionist thinking, or who have hyper-sensitive souls, may be difficult.

Famous Moon in Sagittarius people: Albert Einstein, Oprah Winfrey, Al Pacino, Freddie Mercury, Mike Tyson, Tiger Woods, Lenny Kravitz, Joan Rivers, Jeff Goldblum, Tim Robbins, Vin Diesel, Donald Trump, Steven King

Moon in Capricorn

Moon in Capricorn is in the Moon's *detriment*[13]. The opposite of Cancer, Capricorn is about working towards goals, usually career goals. This focus on work may be at the expense of proper nourishment. This restriction is usually based on the relationship with the mother who in most cases is distant. However, working and handling business are important to the Moon in Capricorn, so this is what they chose. All of the other stuff can wait.

Ruled by Saturn, there may be a severe restriction on what they eat. They may follow a strict, rigid diet. Not one to get emotional, the Moon in Capricorn native approaches issues through a lens of pragmatism. Saturn also indicates there may be a delay, or that it can take a long time for the native to really open up emotionally in an intimate relationship. In many cases, this is due to having a distant relationship with the mother.

What this means for the Moon in Capricorn native:
Moon in Capricorn natives have a fear of intimacy that has to be conquered. Working and career is important, but they shouldn't forget to nurture themselves.

The Moon in Capricorn Comfort Zone:
Like Moon in Cancer they also like a secure home. They prefer stable routines and feel the need to work even when on vacation. Intimacy with someone who is very independent and aggressive, or someone who is too detached and passive, may be a problem.

Famous Moon in Capricorn people: Brad Pitt, George Clooney, Johnny Depp, Matt Damon, Arnold Schwarzenegger, Amy Winehouse, Seal, Andrew Garfield, Sarah Silverman, Robert F. Kennedy, Al Gore.

---

[13] Weakest sign for a planet to be in. Think of detriment planets as away teams, playing in a home team's stadium in weather conditions they're not used to.

Moon in Aquarius

Moon in Aquarius is an interesting moon. As a universal sign, Aquarius is interested in the whole. So Aquarius "feels" for humanity in an abstract way. Usually emotive, affection is channeled into an art form, or activism. Aquarian Moons, because of this inclination to relate to abstract humanity, feel isolated or "odd" because they feel unable to relate to people on a more intimate level. Aquarian Moons feel most comfortable in a crowd, or as a part of a greater whole.

Confrontation, especially in emotional instances, send these natives into retreat. Aquarius doesn't want to wade through mucky emotions and, as a "civilized" universal air sign, would rather avoid conflict and emotional scenes if possible. If stressed, the Moon here can affect nerves and eyes.

What this means for the Moon in Aquarius native:
Moon in Aquarius natives are comfortable with intellectual exchange and a meeting of the minds in an intimate setting. Indulging their senses is important as well, so they shouldn't neglect that aspect of themselves.

The Moon in Aquarius Comfort Zone:
Moon in Aquarius prefers being amongst friends and sharing ideas and philosophies with others. They actually like being alone too to detach and tend to their intellectual hobby. Space emotionally and physically is vital. Intimacy with a demanding, emotional person, or someone who is very grounded and material focused, may be tough.

Famous Moon in Aquarius people: Britney Spears, John Lennon, Pope Francis, Woody Allen, Russell Crowe, Uma Thurman, Victoria Beckham, Phil Jackson, Greg Popovich, Marvin Hagler, Bruce Willis, Eminem.

Moon in Pisces

Moon in Pisces is fulfilled emotionally through caring for the afflicted and sick. Moon in Pisces is extremely sensitive to the emotional temperature of an environment, and they are susceptible to deep melancholy due to negative world events. Moon in Pisces easily picks up the temperament of others and internalizes, which can adversely affect their health.

Moon in Pisces also loves music and the ideals of love, so music and poetry is soul food for them. They must make sure they stay grounded and get enough sleep (which they enjoy). This is important, too, because they tend to have huge hearts that extend beyond self or family (Cancer) and extend to everyone. So if they aren't grounded and thinking clearly they may be taken advantage of.

What this means for the Moon in Pisces native:
The Moon in Pisces native wants to heal and nurture everyone who needs it. So, it's important they make distinctions between those who truly deserve such help and those who don't. They must create boundaries.

The Moon in Pisces Comfort Zone:
Moon in Pisces is most comfortable in seclusion and solitude someplace quiet, especially at night. They need quiet so they can dream and allow their imaginations to run wild. Close emotional intimacy is important to them, but Intimacy with someone who is too talkative, or someone who is very active and blunt, can be an issue.

Famous Moon in Pisces people: Michelle Obama, Michael Jackson, Kim Kardashian, Hillary Clinton, Paul Walker, Robert De Niro, Ben Stiller, Ricky Martin, Kanye West, Prince, Robin Williams, Morgan Freeman, Axl Rose, Jason Statham.

Final Thoughts on Moon Signs

The Sun and the Moon are the most important puzzle pieces in forming an individual's astrological temperament. How they aspect[14] each other will answers many questions about our individual nature. We will explore more specific angles and aspects in the next book.

---

[14] The angle two planets are on in relation to each other in a zodiac dial/natal chart.

-3-

Mercury: The Communicator

As we take more steps into the depths of astrology, we should remember that every planet is a component of the individual. Due to Mercury's proximity to earth, Mercury can only be in the same sign, the following sign, or previous sign as the Sun. Mercury's orbit takes 88 solar days to complete, so Mercury changes signs every 12 days. It's the closest celestial body to the Sun and the body with the shortest orbit after the Moon from Earth's perspective. In astrology, the planet Mercury presides over communication style and thought process, so knowing Mercury's position in the natal chart tells us much about how a person will think through information and interact with others.

Mercury in Aries

In Aries, Mercury is quick to the punch. This is a quick thinking and acting Mercury placement. This is not a position for reflective thinking or calculated speech. Mercury here will speak without thinking. The point of view is highly subjective since Aries is the first personal sign. The energy of Mars drives the communications of these individuals so they are usually very direct and get to the point. Mercury in Aries does not read subtlety and nuance necessarily well.

What this means for Mercury in Aries:
Firing off at the mouth could land a Mercury in Aries in trouble. They should use this quick and direct wit for positive things.

> ➤ <u>Communication Style & Thought Process:</u> Impulsive and direct. Well applied patience and vetting of information will help this placement.

Famous Mercury in Aries people: Al Pacino, Mark Zuckerberg, Mariah Carey, Robert Downey Jr., Charlie Chaplin, Marlon Brando, Vince Vaughn, Patricia Arquette, Marvin Gaye, Shaquille O'Neal, Nat King Cole, Harvey Keitel, Suge Knight.

Mercury in Taurus

Mercury in Taurus is grounded in their thinking. They're the ones to think before they speak, and their speech is slower paced. They also can take longer than other placements at digesting new information.

Once an opinion is held, it's tough to get a Mercury in Taurus to change directions (fixed sign). They have a mind for handling money and managing assets. They are not necessarily a big verbal communicator, but, as a Venus sign, they are capable of charm and generally have a pleasant voice.

<u>What this means for Mercury in Taurus:</u>
They think logically and are sensible, but they shouldn't get stuck in one way of thinking. It is better to vet new information and accept it into their thought process.

> ➤ <u>Communication Style & Thought Process:</u> Practical and tempered. Relies on facts and what appeals to their senses.

Famous Mercury in Taurus people: Johnny Depp, George Clooney, Megan Fox, Kanye West, Jay Leno, Miles Davis, Seth Rogan, George Carlin, George H.W. Bush, Pierce Brosnan, Bono, David Beckham, Naomi Campbell.

Mercury in Gemini

Mercury in Gemini is home for Mercury and where it operates at full strength. Therefore, these individuals can be exceptional speakers and skilled writers. They process information very quickly. They can logically assess, analyze, and relay information. They are not necessarily great conversationalists because they tend to be very subjective. Mercury in Gemini individuals have a good grasp of language. They are capable of gossip since Gemini is a sign that is interested in learning and digesting new information.

What this means for Mercury in Gemini:
They are quick thinkers, and chatting and joking come to them naturally. They usually have a good grasp of language.

> ➢ Communication Style & Thought Process: Quick witted, sharp, and logical. Learns through reading, and human communication.

Famous Mercury in Gemini people: Marv Albert, Mike Breen, Newt Gingrich, Tom Bergeron, Tupac Shakur, Jadakiss, Angelina Jolie, Meryl Streep, Prince, Bob Dylan, 50 cent, Liam Neeson, Lauryn Hill, Melanie Brown, Billy Joel, Chris Brown.

Mercury in Cancer

Mercury in Cancer is the final personal sign for Mercury. These individuals have a powerful photographic memory that goes far back in time. They learn by osmosis. Their frame of reference is highly personal and subjective. They may be very quiet and subdued until they feel ready to speak. The challenge for them is gathering facts and a clear perspective on events.

What this means for Mercury in Cancer:
Their early childhood teachings stay with them. It's important for Mercury

in Cancer not to cling to those old ways of thinking if they are not helping them progress in life.

> Communication Style & Thought Process: Reflective and relies on personal experiences as a frame of reference when learning something new.

Famous Mercury in Cancer people: Carl Jung, Harrison Ford, Ariana Grande, Tom Hanks, Arnold Schwarzenegger, Will Ferrell, Zoe Saldana, Vin Diesel, Jason Statham, Pamela Anderson, Bill Cosby, Hulk Hogan, Louis Armstrong.

Mercury in Leo

Mercury in Leo is the creative thinker—a thinker who operates from a very artistic place. Leo is a fixed sign so they will stubbornly stick to something they believe despite evidence to the contrary. Since Leo is a fire sign there is an inclination to jump to conclusions and use hyperbole. They may be extremely inspirational speakers, able to spark the passions of listeners. They want to speak authoritatively and in a grandiose way about whatever they may be talking about. This is a placement of the thespian.

What this means for Mercury in Leo:
They are creative, demonstrative and charismatic speakers. It's important for them, however, to engage in two-way communication and not bring the topic focal point to themselves exclusively.

> Communication Style & Thought Process: Ego-centered and flamboyant. Learns through their experiences.

Famous Mercury in Leo people: Barack Obama, Michael Jackson, Jennifer Lopez, Bill Clinton, George W. Bush, Halle Berry, Nelson Mandela, Mick Jagger, J.K. Rowling, Kobe Bryant, Mike Tyson, Charlie Sheen.

Mercury in Virgo

Mercury in Virgo is the first interpersonal Mercury sign and is home like Mercury in Gemini. However Mercury in Virgo is an Earth Mercury and, unlike Mercury in Gemini, is focused on tangibility. The ability to be a skilled speaker is usually present, but there is less of a focus on abstracts. Mercury in Virgo is mechanically inclined and looks for errors and small details to fix. They can be very critical and look for errors to a point that others may find irritating.

What this means for Mercury in Virgo:
They understand the components of a machination and can articulate how it works. They know what errors to point out when a particular system is not working. They should be sure to not only speak about faults and give critiques but also offer solutions and ways to improve.

> ➤ Communication Style & Thought Process: Practical, analytical, and critical. Mercury in Virgo learns through physical application of process and repetition.

Famous Mercury in Virgo people: Amy Winehouse, Whitney Houston, Robert De Niro, Pink, Coco Chanel, Sting, Alfred Hitchcock, Emmy Rossum, Nick Jonas, Kylie Jenner, Bill Murray, Tom Brady, Damon Wayans, Ludacris, Paul Walker.

Mercury in Libra

Mercury in Libra is a thoughtful tactician. Venus softens the vocal tone of these individuals. Like Taurus, there is a kind of a slow and calculating way they communicate. They have a natural musical inclination and their voices usually have a pleasing tone.

Mercury in Libra has the ability to see all sides of an issue. As an air Mercury sign, they are exceptionally communicative and keen socializers.

They have the ability to focus on pleasantries and overlook what may be seen as flaws.

What this means for Mercury in Libra:
They are an "ideas person" and an objective thinker. It's important for them to make concrete decisions and be direct in communication when necessary.

> Communication Style & Thought Process: Measured, tactful, and diplomatic. Learns through reading and in a classic classroom setting. Like Mercury in Taurus, there is a calmness to the way they speak and process information.

Famous Mercury in Libra people: Beyonce Knowles, Leonardo DiCaprio, Nas, Clive Owen, Heather Locklear, Jeremy Irons, Wiz Khalifa, Dr. Phil, Jennifer Hudson, Thelonius Monk, Evander Holyfield, Napoleon Hill, Rita Wilson, Larry Flynt.

Mercury in Scorpio

Mercury in Scorpio is a quiet contemplative Mercury placement. They watch and observe before they speak. These are the detectives. Mercury in Scorpios generally have strong concentration powers and have the intuitive ability to read between the lines. They also will hang on to an idea very tightly and will not budge from their positions when challenged. These people are good photographic and visual learners, much like Cancer.

What this means for Mercury in Scorpio:
There is a suspicious nature to their thoughts. They tend to keep a wealth of details to themselves whether they be secrets or strategically withheld information.

> ➢ <u>Communication Style & Thought Process</u>: Penetrating, intuitive, and persistent. Mercury in Scorpios, like Mercury in Cancer, draw from the feelings of a specific memory and that guides them in new situations. Mercury in Scorpio is concrete in decision making. Once their mind is made, it's not going to be changed willingly.

Famous Mercury in Scorpio People: Jodie Foster, Julia Roberts, Ciara, Owen Wilson, David Guetta, Deepak Chopra, Eminem, Katy Perry, Hillary Duff, Meg Ryan, Grace Kelly, Whoopi Goldberg.

Mercury in Sagittarius

Mercury in Sagittarius is in detriment. The detail-oriented nature of Mercury is counter to Sagittarius's big picture outlook. These individuals often make fantastic comedians. Quick witted and sharp, they often shift focus quickly (mutable fire) mid-sentence to change the direction of a conversation. Their weakness is dealing with mundane details. Mercury in Sagittarius believes that integrity and justice is important. They think in sweeping moral terms, so what makes sense pragmatically or logically is not necessarily what comes to mind to them organically.

<u>What this means for Mercury in Sagittarius:</u>
They think and speak in a spirited way and have strong beliefs, but they shouldn't let those beliefs override facts when inappropriate.

> ➢ <u>Communication Style & Thought Process</u>: Holistic, quick witted, and blunt. Mercury in Sagittarius processes and communicates the main idea of a thought but tends to miss many of the details, some of which can be very important.

Famous Mercury in Sagittarius People: Jon Stewart, Woody Allen, Jude Law, Britney Spears, Jay-Z, Jamie Foxx, Redd Foxx, Patrice O'Neil, Nicki

Minaj, Jeff Bridges, Jeremy Renner, Jake Gyllenhaal, Maggie Gyllenhaal, Mary J. Blige.

Mercury in Capricorn

Mercury in Capricorn individuals are linear thinkers. Ruled by Saturn, they think along conventional lines. Mercury here likes to think things through before they speak because there is a need to be sure of their knowledge and present it in a refined way. Mercury in Capricorn has a mind for managerial duties and seeing how all moving parts in a system should be operating together, so they are good at compartmentalization. Because Capricorn is ruled by Saturn, they tend to be critical and can be pessimistic. Mercury in Capricorn people usually have a monotone voice.

What this means for Mercury in Capricorn:
Mercury in Capricorn thinks and speaks in a very systematic and practical way. They should try to be open to new ideas.

> ➢ Communication Style & Thought Process: Linear, grounded, and definitive. Mercury in Capricorn is a hands-on practical learner.

Famous Mercury in Capricorn People: Michelle Obama, Brad Pitt, Samuel L. Jackson, DMX, Joseph Stalin, Shakira, Ellen DeGeneres, Bradley Cooper, Jane Fonda, Al Capone, J.R.R. Tolkein, Howard Stern, R. Kelly, Michael C. Hall.

Mercury in Aquarius

Mercury in Aquarius is the computer scientist and objectivist. As an air sign, they can be chatty. They look for a universal truth in most situations. Their mind works quickly and you might hear them utter something shockingly witty and funny out of the blue. They understand holistic concepts as a universal sign[15], see the big picture objectively, and can articulate complex issues. They are the public speaker who, backed with numbers and statistics, can explain these systems to large crowds, for example, Steve Jobs.

<u>What this means for Mercury in Aquarius:</u>
They are "book smart" and understand communicating the big picture. They are socially adept, so communications is a good field for them to get into.

> ➤ <u>Communication Style & Thought Process</u>: Objective, rational, and detached. Thought process is logical.

Famous Mercury in Aquarius People: Rihanna, Justin Bieber, Eva Mendes, Sarah Palin, Jennifer Aniston, Martin Luther King Jr., Steve Jobs, Alicia Keys, Muhammed Ali, Kevin Costner, Chris Rock, LL Cool J, Oprah Winfrey, Jim Carrey.

Mercury in Pisces

Mercury in Pisces is in detriment. Mercury in Pisces individuals' thought process is murky due to Pisces' dreamy and intuitive nature. They are inclined to have a photographic and tonal memory. They recognize sounds and sights more so than words. Their negative traits include a tendency to exaggerate or outright lie and do so convincingly. Their mind works like a vast ocean, picking up on specific sounds (like a one-on-one conversation) while also picking up garbage (so to speak). This added "noise" is what makes their thinking a bit muddled. Pisces is about higher spirituality which doesn't always easily translate into the right words. So, to someone

---

[15] Last 4 signs of the zodiac, also known as the transpersonal signs. Their planet rulers are planets that rule over events and ideas beyond the individual, but that have influence on the totality of society.

without knowledge of Astrology, this person might not appear too smart, but they have just as much intellectual capacity as any other Mercury; it's just expressed differently.

<u>What this means for Mercury in Pisces:</u>
Mercury in Pisces is in tune with music and art and has a great mind for those mediums. They don't necessarily communicate well verbally, though. Emotions color their thought process, so it's important they be in a comfortable environment and focused if they have to speak publically. It is advantageous for these natives to take public speaking courses or get involved with some type of public speaking club or group.

> ➤ <u>Communication Style & Thought Process</u>: Murky, inspired, photographic, and non-linear.

Famous Mercury In Pisces People: Lady Gaga, Sharon Stone, Heath Ledger, Kurt Cobain, Johnny Cash, Pharell Williams, Chuck Norris, Eddie Murphy, Mitt Romney, John Travolta, Jackie Chan, Eckhart Tolle, David Letterman, Robin Thicke.

Final Thoughts on Mercury signs

Now that you know your core (Sun sign), your emotional comfort zone (Moon Sign), and thought process (Mercury), you can look at these individual pieces of your *natal chart* and gain a more targeted understanding of how you function.

-4-

Love (Venus)

The planet Venus reveals how we express love, relate to others, and what we should expect in our partners. As we piece this puzzle together, it's important to note that Venus can only be 60 degrees, or 2 signs away from your Sun. So for example if you were born on August 29ᵗʰ which is Virgo, you would only be able to have Venus in Cancer, Leo, Virgo, Libra, or Scorpio. Venus takes 225 days to orbit and spends 18 ½ days in each sign.

Venus is a man's ideal woman

Venus indicates the type of woman a man tends to be attracted to as well. So men reading this should check out this placement and see if their significant other has the corresponding Sun sign, or has it as an ascendant sign (I will go through ascendant signs in the next book).

Venus in Aries

Venus in Aries is in detriment, as Aries is a conqueror and counter to the nature of Venus. Venus in Aries is interested in action in a relationship. This person mostly considers their own potential for gain and focuses on their own needs in a relationship. Aries is a fire sign, so jumping into a relationship based on passion and excitement alone is the norm for these individuals. However, there is a tendency to become bored when things calm down and normalize. Unlike Venus in Libra who sees a relationship as a collaboration, Venus in Aries sees it as a competition.

What this means for Venus in Aries:
They relate with enthusiasm and passion, but have to remember the other person's needs as well.

> How Venus in Aries relates: Enthusiasm, asserting their own will. Relating aggressively.

Famous Venus in Aries People: Rihanna, Mariah Carey, Jennifer Aniston, Steven Seagal, Eddie Murphy, Janet Jackson, Morgan Freeman, Bobby Brown, Jack Nicholson, Robert Downey Jr., Bob Marley, Lady Gaga.

Venus in Taurus

Venus in Taurus is in domicile as Taurus is ruled by Venus. Venus in Taurus loves money, physical comforts and owning possessions of value. Good food, money and the sense of touch are their lifeblood. As a fixed sign, they want their relationships to be stable and they like a degree of control over their lover.

Venus in Taurus' possessions may include their significant other. Wearing comfortable clothes is important in contrast to the aesthetic fashion desires of a Libra. Venus in Taurus appreciates sexual pleasures, but not just sex. They value the entire love making process. Taurus rules money, so Venus in Taurus does a good job at attracting money. Also, because of the earth element, they know how to store money, so, unlike Jupiter-ruled signs, they have a better idea how to hang on to it.

What this means for Venus in Taurus:
Venus in Taurus has the ability to build wealth and accumulate possessions. They are in touch with the physical world. Change in relationships is difficult for this placement. They should accept change as it comes. They're inclined towards business, especially the culinary arts.

> ➢ How Venus in Taurus relates: Sharing possessions, sense of touch and other sensual pleasures.

Famous Venus in Taurus People: Johnny Depp, Kanye West, Chuck Norris, Mark Zuckerberg, James Franco, Chris Brown, Paul McCartney, Bono, Prince, Michael J. Fox, Lisa Lopes, George Lucas, Cillian Murphy, Jessica Alba.

Venus in Gemini

Venus in Gemini enjoys communication in relationships and leisure. As a personal sign, Venus in Gemini tends not to be as concerned with what their partner is saying, but they need an active listener. Lively get-togethers with witty conversation and open, unrestricted thought and communication are what they enjoy.

Since Gemini is an air sign, physical presence isn't always a necessity. Texts and phone calls are important reassurances for Venus in Gemini. Another favorite past time for many of these natives is reading.

What this means for Venus in Gemini:
Calling people and texting is what they enjoy most. They should not neglect other forms of relating however. It is important for them to indulge in physical pleasures and emotional intimacy as well to keep balance.

> ➢ How Venus in Gemini relates: Open communication, joking, writing. Mental rapport is extremely important.

Famous Venus in Gemini People: Russell Crowe, Jennifer Lopez, Nelson Mandela, Heidi Klum, Tom Hanks, Channing Tatum, Liam Neeson, Jerry Seinfeld, Tina Fey, Malcolm X, Joan Rivers, Mike Tyson, William Shakespeare.

Venus in Cancer

Venus in Cancer loves the virtues of family, and close friends, so they like to keep their circles smaller. They tend to have a strong bond with their mothers and they relate best on a one-to-one basis or in small groups in a social setting. Cancer loves good food, so a family dinner party might be a Venus in Cancer's favorite event. So would be eating out at a local hole in the wall restaurant.

Cancer is an auspicious sign for money, and a Venus in Cancer may have a small family business operation, something that is keen on the needs of people. They like to hold onto possessions and accumulate money for security. Venus in Cancer isn't going to share a loved one. For them, physical and emotional intimacy is important and that includes physical proximity. Water signs have keenly accurate intuition, so these natives will know if things aren't quite right.

What this means for Venus in Cancer:
They relate to others very intimately. If they're a woman, they're likely much closer with women than they are with men.

> How Venus in Cancer relates: Intimacy, sharing food, physical contact, and nurturing. Venus in Cancer, like Moon in Cancer usually has a strong connection with their mother. This mother archetype is what informs their method of caring for their significant others.

Famous Venus in Cancer people: Barack Obama, Melanie Brown, Angelina Jolie, Ben Affleck, Clint Eastwood, Halle Berry, Jack Black, Hulk Hogan, Anderson Cooper, Edward Norton, Russell Brand, Nikola Tesla, Lenny Kravitz.

Venus in Leo

Venus in Leo is prideful and enjoys attention in relationships. They appreciate grand gestures of affection. They take pride in their romantic partners. They are a fixed sign, so remaining the main object of affection and attention is very important to them. They may become upset if they think someone else is getting too much attention or "outshines" them. They want to be number #1 in the relationship. Venus in Leo wants to share themselves with the public or social circles in a creative way, whether through art, fashion, theater, or other creative mediums. Their creativity has a flamboyant flair to it.

What this means for Venus in Leo:
They have a lot of pride and love to impress people. They want a spouse they can show off and be proud of, but they want to be the centerpiece of the relationship.

> ➤ How Venus in Leo relates: Romance, kinship, sex, and creativity. Wants to impress their significant other.

Famous Venus in Leo people: Madonna, Michael Jackson, Amy Winehouse, Whitney Houston, 50 Cent, Salma Hayek, Tom Cruise, George W. Bush, Dave Navarro, Tyler Perry, Kelis, Nicole Kidman.

Venus in Virgo

Venus in Virgo is in fall. This means that the luxuries Venus enjoys are given conditions by Virgo. Venus in Virgo loves through service, caring for, and nursing a loved one. If the Venus in Virgo individual isn't sure where to channel that energy, there may be a lot of criticism and attempts to fix seemingly trivial problems. This placement shows that there is guilt at times in relationships for not being perfect and living up to their own personal expectations

<u>What this means for Venus in Virgo:</u>
They are supportive, but in a critical way. They should learn to reinforce others with encouragement as much as critique. They are inclined towards technical fields like engineering and medical science.

> <u>How Venus in Virgo relates</u>: Serving their significant other, indulging in sensual pleasures. Partnership based in practicality more so than emotional connection.

Famous Venus in Virgo people: Eminem, Robin Williams, Kim Kardashian, J.K. Rowling, Antonio Banderas, Mila Kunis, Robert De Niro, Gwen Stefani, Robert Redford, Julia Roberts, Kylie Jenner, Kevin Spacey, Jimmy Fallon.

Venus in Libra

Venus in Libra is in domicile because Libra is also a cerebral air sign. This is a social sign though, and Venus in Libra is keenly aware of other's needs and especially aware of their partner's needs. Doing things in pairs is something Libra enjoys. Even if they're not paired with their spouse, they like to be partnered with somebody while going out and about.

Similar to the other Venus air signs, open communication is important. Venus helps the tactful Libra to be able to choose the right things to say at the right time. Libra tends to be in love with love though, and Venus may withhold information if they believe it will hurt their partner or their partnership.

Venus in Libra is keener than Venus in Gemini when it comes to the back and forth social exchange, so Venus in Libra may not shoot off at the mouth like Venus in Gemini .

<u>What this means for Venus in Libra:</u>
They want to get along with people and try to be fair in all their dealings. They are adept at judging balance and fairness in social interactions. Venus

in Libra should attempt not to bend over backwards at their own expense, however. This can lead to others taking advantage of their need to be fair.

> ➢ <u>How Venus in Libra relates</u>: Sharing and through cooperation, being attentive. Going out and about socializing as a couple.

Famous Venus in Libra people: Bill Clinton, Beyonce Knowles, Grace Kelly, Will Smith, Jada Pinkett Smith, Woody Allen, Paul Walker, Dave Chappelle, Michael Douglas, Lisa Bonet, Puff Daddy, Jim Henson.

Venus in Scorpio

Scorpio is in Venus's detriment because Scorpio is Mars-ruled. Therefore, the qualities of Venus that many other signs enjoy only operate on the extremes of Scorpio. Scorpio is a sign of transformation, conquest, and power. Venus in Scorpio goes to extremes since Venus isn't balanced and fluid here. Where Venus in Aries wants to conquer physically, Venus in Scorpio wants to feel in control psychologically and spiritually; therefore, intensity and intimacy is very important and trust is a huge factor.

Venus in Scorpio likes to keep a circle of friends that is trustworthy and reliable, people who are not afraid of raw honesty and who can be crude. Opposite to Taurus, which indicates personal wealth and possessions, Scorpio rules over other people's possessions. Thus, Venus in Scorpio is adept at making money through assisting other people. Venus in Scorpio also enjoys power, so they may open themselves up to new circles if it means there is a position of prestige or authority that is up for grabs. This placement is not really known as much for its creativity; they tend to be more adept at business.

<u>What this means for Venus in Scorpio:</u>
They are intense and may be overzealous in their pursuit once they feel it's ok to do so. They likely choose to be very quiet until they trust those around them. It is important for them to try to keep a balanced perspective

and not smother their significant other. Setting up an arrangement where the couple sleeps in two separate bedrooms might be very advantageous to the Venus in Scorpio.

> How Venus in Scorpio relates: Intense interactions that excite them emotionally. Emotional and sexual bonding is top priority. Engaging in taboo activities.

Famous Venus in Scorpio people: Leonardo DiCaprio, Denzel Washington, Jodie Foster, Nas, Bruce Lee, Jim Morrison, Steven Spielberg, Bill Gates, Ted Turner, Jane Fonda, Ray Liotta, Vladimir Putin, Snoop Dogg, Serena Williams, Kris Jenner.

Venus in Sagittarius

Venus in Sagittarius is likely to have a relationship with someone of a different race, ethnicity, or religion. They are open-hearted and open-minded for the most part. They trust their partners which may be taken advantage of. Since Sagittarius is a mutable sign, there may be periodic urges to venture out of their current relationship. Venus in Sagittarius wants their romance to be a fun ride with plenty of activity while learning together. They are likely to have a wide array of friends in many different places both near and far. This might be the placement that's most interested in a long-distance relationship.

What this means for Venus in Sagittarius:
They have a friendly and jovial way of socializing. They enjoy the company of people from different backgrounds. A lover relationship with someone of another race, ethnicity, or religion.

> How Venus in Sagittarius relates: Excitement, shared learning experiences. Traveling as a couple.

Famous Venus in Sagittarius people: Nicki Minaj, Katy Perry, Samuel L. Jackson, Tina Turner, Joseph Stalin, Jake Gyllenhaal, Kendall Jenner, Bruce Jenner, Jeff Goldblum, Rita Ora, Whoopi Goldberg, Jimi Hendrix.

Venus in Capricorn

Venus in Capricorn is not the most openly affectionate and gregarious Venus. In truth, they can be pretty reserved, especially if they're around unfamiliar people they aren't really sure about. Venus in Capricorn is not very comfortable with flamboyant PDA and, in general, they are not huge fans of a lot of "Lovey-dovey" or sappy affection, except for in the bedroom or around family they're comfortable with. Venus in Capricorn natives will express their love through doing tasks and give gifts they find practical for the recipient and which will make their life easier and more comfortable. Do not embarrass them. Providing stability financially is important.

Venus in Capricorn is much more of a spendthrift than Venus in Taurus. They don't necessarily attract money as easily as the benefic-ruled Venus signs. So they work for it and therefore don't want to part ways with it very easily.

What this means for Venus in Capricorn:
They like to plan ahead before social outings. They appreciate order, structure, and goals in their relationships. It is important to mix things up, though, and at time do something totally new and spontaneous.

> ➢ How Venus in Capricorn relates: Sharing gifts, doing favors in the form of work, providing physical and financial security. Social outings with close and trusted friends.

Famous Venus in Capricorn people: Brad Pitt, Scarlett Johansson, Mylie Cyrus, Tyra Banks, Frank Sinatra, Bradley Cooper, Ben Stiller, Dolly Parton, Owen Wilson, Lucy Liu, Jeff Bridges, Howard Stern, Seal.

Venus in Aquarius

Venus in Aquarius is a universal air sign. As such, Venus in Aquarius is concerned with ideals and abstract concepts that affect humanity. This care for humanity usually comes with a struggle with one-on-one relationships. For them, open communication with groups, whether colleagues or friends, is important. Venus in Aquarius tends to take Venus in Gemini's love of communication a step further and takes this communication knack to the group setting. Social gatherings in a group setting is how they like to spend leisure time, either that or being alone engaged with something intellectual.

This is someone who probably loves Skyping or group video chats. Their loved one may be of a different culture and live elsewhere altogether, but as long as Skype works, they will be fine. Venus in Aquarius will likely settle down with one person if they are the embodiment of one of their abstract ideals. It will just take a bit of time since the fixed signs tend to move slowly.

<u>What this means for Venus in Aquarius:</u>
They will socialize with just about anyone without judgement but want to remain unrestrained by others. They want freedom of movement but not necessarily change in relationships.

➢ <u>How Venus in Aquarius relates</u>: Socializing, communicating by phone or Internet, exchanging ideas.

Famous Venus in Aquarius people: Bruce Willis, Paris Hilton, Mel Gibson, Mitt Romney, Eva Mendes, Gary Oldman, Elton John, Sade Adu, Lebron James, R. Kelly, Tony Robbins, Taylor Swift, Sharon Stone.

Venus in Pisces

Venus in Pisces is exalted. The yin qualities of Jupiter help this placement bring good fortune to the native. Pisces rules art, music, film, and photography, so these fields are where Venus in Pisces can make a good living. The open nature of Pisces allows for a rich inner world of fantasy that can translate into some incredible art.

Pisces, again, is a universal sign that cares for more than simply the immediate family and a small circle of friends as with Cancer and Scorpio. They have a concern for everyone, including animals. As a mutable sign this placement may not be as reliable or consistent as Venus in Cancer or Scorpio, but that's because a Piscean's nature is versatile and flexible. They are one of the caretakers of the zodiac, and, as such, they can't do their duty if they are too forward moving (Cardinal) or dominant (Fixed). Venus in Pisces is good at making money through charity, but also susceptible to spending and giving it all away. If there are needy friends or family, they won't hesitate to provide what is needed.

What this means for Venus in Pisces:
They are charitable and giving. They shouldn't let people take advantage of them however. Strong boundaries should be maintained.

> ➢ How Venus in Pisces relates: Service and giving of themselves freely. Empathy, intimacy. Non-judgement of others. Emotional intimacy.

Famous Venus in Pisces people: Bill Maher, Martin Luther King Jr., Michelle Obama, Heath Ledger, Lucy Lawless, Ronald Reagan, Norah Jones, Patricia Arquette, Rod Stewart, Richard Nixon, Diana Ross, Jon Bon Jovi, Edgar Cayce.

-5-
War (Mars)

Just as we love and relate to others, we have causes and goals that motivate us and push us into action. This motivation many times puts us in direct contention with others. Whether it be offenses committed against one another or healthy competition, as in sports. We all have this spirit within us, but we as individuals have different ways of expressing that spirit and different motivating factors. In astrology, the planet Mars and its sign placement tell us what factors are behind our particular motivations. Mars is the burst of fiery energy needed to start a war. Mars is action, but it is also sex and how it is pursued. In a woman's chart, her Mars sign shows us what type of man brings out her passion. Mars takes 687 days to orbit, so each sign takes 58 days to travel through.

Mars is a woman's ideal man

The qualities of a woman's Mars sign show what type of man draws out her passion. It does not necessarily have to be a man of that sign. But someone who embodies those characteristics will draw her attention.

Mars in Aries

The first zodiac sign, Aries, is ruled by Mars, so of course Mars begins in Aries. Mars is the god of war and Aries is the cardinal sign genesis of the new year, representing a burst of new life. Mars placed here will be full of vitality as well as direct and assertive. Mars in Aries has a fiery impulse, so they are prone to quick bursts of anger, although they are just as quickly and easily calmed down. On the negative side, they can be inconsiderate and overbearing, lacking patience and consideration of others.

Mars in Aries will initiate new ventures without much planning. Instead, they will act on intuition and impulse, which is pretty good for the most part. They make for good athletes as well.

<u>What this means for Mars in Aries:</u>
They are self-motivated and quick-tempered. They go after what they want aggressively. This assertiveness can lead to accidents. This is a strong primal force, but in modern society tact is needed. So it's important to know when to be assertive and when to hold back.

> <u>Mars in Aries Motivations</u>: Personal needs and goals. Strong sexual desires. Winning is important, so is fighting for their honor.

Famous Mars in Aries people: Russell Crowe, Tyra Banks, Steve Jobs, Andre 3000, Angelina Jolie, Larry Bird, Paul Newman, Claire Daines, Melanie Brown, Cristiano Ronaldo, Kevin Costner, Emma Stone, Prince, Tobey McGuire.

Mars in Taurus

Mars in Taurus is in Mars' detriment, meaning Mars here is ruled by Venus and motivated by sensuality and physical comforts as opposed to conquests and battles. An enjoyable time, good food, sex, and money are what motivates Mars in Taurus. Mars here can be lazy and indolent, but, when motivated, has the singularity of purpose and willpower of other fixed signs. If the money is good they will work very hard.

Mars in Taurus individuals are usually slow moving but exceptionally strong. At their core, they love peace and comfort and have a very long fuse, but, if pushed far enough, they will blow that fuse. This is a good placement for business and accumulating wealth.

<u>What this means for Mars in Taurus:</u>
They like to take it easy and enjoy sensuality. They are slow to get themselves into action, but they don't let this tendency stop them from reaching goals.

> Mars in Taurus Motivations: Physical pleasure and enjoyment. Good food. Making money, especially through ownership of possessions that appreciate in value.

Famous Mars in Taurus people: Bruce Willis, Tom Cruise, Mick Jagger, Robert De Niro, Paul Walker, Christian Bale, Muhammed Ali, 50 Cent, Jamie Lee Curtis, Sade Adu, Kate Moss, Lenny Kravitz, Chuck Norris.

Mars in Gemini

Mars in Gemini natives have mental energy to spare. Lower mind activities or what could be considered left brain activities, like writing, word games, and human interaction, keep these restless-minded individuals' attention. Quick-witted and sharp-minded, these natives are excited by the chance to match wits.

Although Mars in Gemini may be adept at using their hands, they need to be mentally stimulated to do physical work. For them, this restlessness and short attention span can be a problem as well as fickle behavior and empty words. Mars in Gemini individuals assert themselves through conversation, spoken, and written word which could lead to arguments if angered. When angered, they use their words to sting.

<u>What this means for Mars in Gemini:</u>
They need mental stimulus to take physical action. They use words to assert themselves more so than physical force. As a Mars in air sign, it is important to hold yourself to your words and put action behind them. Mars in air signs may become content with simply thinking and not acting.

> ➤ Mars in Gemini Motivations: Learning and education. Conversation and social interaction.

Famous Mars in Gemini people: Mike Tyson, Jim Morrison, Arnold Schwarzenegger, Al Pacino, Sean Penn, Martin Luther King Jr., Meryl Streep, Sandra Bullock, Helen Mirren, Tom Brady, Tina Fey, Damon Wayans.

Mars in Cancer

Mars in Cancer is in Mars' fall. Mars is assertive and Cancer is a retiring energy. Energy and actions taken will depend largely on comfort zone and the Moon's current transits (Moon cycle). Not comfortable being directly aggressive or assertive, Mars here can be passive aggressive with emotionally driven actions. Even so, this Mars is good for sports.

When a Mars in Cancer's home, loved ones, or family is threatened, they will go to great lengths to protect them. However, when making life decisions, Mars in Cancer will test the waters first. If the water is a comfortable temperature and *feels* safe, that is when Mars in Cancer will move forward.

What this means for Mars in Cancer:
They take action into new and unknown challenges only when they *feel* comfortable and reassured. They are more indirect than direct which can be confusing for both them and the people they interact with throughout the course of their lives. Channeling this energy into helping others will likely be worthwhile. Cancer is a maternal energy, so hospitality fields may be inspiring and motivating for them.

> ➤ Mars in Cancer Motivations: Intimacy and emotional connection. Eating. Protection of family and/or those closest to them.

Famous Mars in Cancer people: Eddie Murphy, Terry Crews, Lionel Messi, Keanu Reeves, Alan Rickman, Pink, Robin Williams, Chris Brown, Tom

Hardy, Novak Djokavic, Ray Charles, Kathy Griffin, Richard Gere, Halle Berry.

Mars in Leo

Mars in Leo people are usually very passionate, opinionated, and full of pride. They really want to be respected, so they will pursue ventures ardently and with unwavering will power. With the vibrant energy of the Sun propelling them, one can expect to see them out ahead of the pack leading the way, rather than trailing behind. They will be generous and lively with the ones they truly love and will work to impress them. On the negative side, they exhibit extreme egocentricity and ignorance to others opinions or advice, as they tend to think their way is the best way to tackle goals. They also may act entitled and may have bouts of laziness. However their energy levels are high and steady. This is an excellent placement for athletics.

<u>What this means for Mars in Leo:</u>
They take bold action, especially when they can impress other people. They are assertive, and, when anyone challenges their reputation, they respond quickly.

> ➢ <u>Mars in Leo Motivations</u>: Prospect of glory and attention. Fulfillment of ego desires.

Famous Mars in Leo people: Harrison Ford, Michael Jordan, Serena Williams, Beyonce Knowles, Cher, Demi Moore, Amy Winehouse, Hakeem Olajuwon, Jerry Rice, George Clooney, Hillary Clinton, James Franco.

Mars in Virgo

Mars in Virgo individuals are usually sharp at spotting mistakes and understanding the mechanics of objects and situations in the physical world. They are motivated by seeing mistakes and disorderly environments and then fixing them. Mars in Virgo wants to serve, so fixing mistakes and tying up loose ends is how Mars in Virgo likes to work.

Because of the Virgo ideal of perfection, these natives may work extremely hard to the point of what looks like obsessive-compulsive behavior to some. Mars in Virgo may be seen in the skilled trades or in the service industry, especially as waiters/waitresses or bartenders.

<u>What this means for Mars in Virgo:</u>
They are motivated by helping others and fixing problems. Work that involves a cross section of service or troubleshooting and technical skills would be something that would keep them interested.

> ➤ Mars in Virgo Motivations: Troubleshooting and fixing all types of errors. Being of service, especially in health-related situations.

Famous Mars in Virgo people: Barack Obama, Bernard Hopkins, Will Smith, Hugh Jackman, Ben Affleck, Britney Spears, Johnny Depp, George W. Bush, Matt Damon, Robert Downey Jr., Derek Fisher, Bruno Mars.

Mars in Libra

Mars in Libra is in detriment. Because Aries is at home in Mars and Libra is the opposite of Aries, Libra here is weakened. Mars in Libra is an individual who constantly weighs options and is very calculating. Ruled by Venus, beauty brings out their passion and many Mars in Libra natives happen to be musicians or musically inclined. They also do well as diplomats and politicians.

There are fluctuating energies here. Some moments, a Mars in Libra may feel they can conquer the world, while at others they may remain very apathetic. They have a need to socialize, and, like other Mars in air signs, keeping their mind active is needed to do physical work. They are energized by social interaction, but they care more about peace and quiet in intense situations. If a situation becomes too intense or event violent they will try to bring it to a peaceful conclusion rather than escalating it. Contrarily, If an environment gets too stagnant, they will bring in some conflict in the form of friendly debate to liven things up.

What this means for Mars in Libra:
They are intellectual fighters. It is important for them to live where they stay in contact with people regularly. They are energized by social interaction. A life where they are isolated can lead to inaction.

> ➤ Mars in Libra Motivations: Socializing and schmoozing. Creation of art or music. Business, negotiation, and strategy development. Bringing two conflicting sides to an agreement.

Famous Mars in Libra people: Bill Gates, Nicole Kidman, Eminem, Kobe Bryant, Nelson Mandela, Whitney Houston, J.K. Rowling, Abraham Lincoln, Kris Jenner, John D. Rockefeller, R. Kelly, Jimmy Fallon, Lucy Liu, Kiefer Sutherland.

Mars in Scorpio

Mars in Scorpio (Fixed Water) is in Mars' domicile. Mars in Scorpio, when engaged, will work towards something with dedication and willpower. Because Scorpio is a feminine water sign, Mars in Scorpio natives aren't quick to reveal their motives. One may never know their intentions until they are angered and unleash their temper. Physically this placement is strong with a very obsessive will.

Scorpio rules the sexual reproductive organs, so anything related to sex will attract a Mars in Scorpio native. However, they are selective and crave intimacy. Mars in Scorpio will hold themselves back from intimacy until they believe the right person comes along and they are vetted as safe, and worthy.

<u>What this means for Mars in Scorpio:</u>
They find something they're drawn to and they pursue it obsessively but in an indirect way. The potential to uncover and obsessively dig and dig for answers to solve mysteries. The power of healing and that potential to heal others also motivates them. Lastly, finding a sexual partner is vital. Only one which they trust to open up emotionally to.

> <u>Mars in Scorpio Motivations</u>: Uncovering hidden truths, Healing and merging souls through sex. To have power in some form.

Famous Mars in Scorpio people: Leonardo DiCaprio, Taylor Swift, Bruce Lee, Jude Law, Mel Gibson, Jimi Hendrix, Mark Zuckerberg, T.I. , Jennifer Aniston, Carmelo Anthony, Morgan Freeman, Bill Murray, Nelly, Jeremy Renner.

Mars in Sagittarius

Mars in Sagittarius gives the native the expansive powers of Thor (Jupiter) to accomplish many different tasks. They are direct people who will give people their honest opinion. Winning a debate may prove to be futile because they will out shout a person if they can't win on facts. They enjoy having fun doing a plethora of things and doing them with enthusiasm (even if they don't finish them all). They are motivated by causes larger than themselves, so religion and spiritual systems are likely to motivate them into action as well.

Due to their mutable nature, there can be some inconsistency to the Mars in Sagittarius native. Sometimes they will be very energetic but follow that energy with a dormant period. On the negative side, they can be reckless and inattentive to detail, resulting in injury. They also take intellectual criticism very personally and fire back with sharp barbs.

What this means for Mars in Sagittarius:
Moral crusades of any magnitude inspire them. They are drawn to learning new things totally unfamiliar to them.

> Mars in Sagittarius Motivations: Faith, new or foreign experiences.

Famous Mars in Sagittarius people: Miguel Cotto, Jennifer Lopez, Rihanna, Bradley Cooper, Kim Kardashian, Vladimir Putin, Jack Nicolson, Meg Ryan, Val Kilmer, Jack Black, Bill Maher, Ice Cube, Paul Rudd.

Mars in Capricorn

Mars is exalted in Capricorn, and Capricorn is ruled by Saturn. This essentially boils down to *assertive* (mars) *working* (Capricorn). Mars in Capricorn is motivated by career results, and, with it being ruled by Saturn, Mars places a burden of responsibility on itself that just motivates the native to work harder and in a very structured and disciplined way. Since Capricorn is an earth sign this work tends to be labor of some sort whether it's as a mechanic or an athlete.

Many successful professional athletes have this placement. Mars in Capricorn is a person who will work hard doing repetitive tasks to further the progression of their enterprise or craft.

What this means for Mars in Capricorn:
They have a strong grasp on the physical world and will work persistently to achieve their goals. They are results oriented people, and take action when they see the steps in front of them.

> Mars in Capricorn Motivations: Seeing positive results from consistent work. Sex and carnal desires. Work itself.

Famous Mars in Capricorn people: Samuel L. Jackson, Nicki Minaj, Lady Gaga, Shakira, Bob Marley, Jim Carrey, Shakira, Brad Pitt, Megan Fox, Ben Stiller, Usain Bolt, Gwen Stefani, Marlon Brando, Julia Roberts.

Mars in Aquarius

Mars in Aquarius is the rebel. Mars in Aquarius natives are the free spirits who buck the status quo consciously and express this in intellectual ways. They excel at revolutionizing existing dynamics by making up new styles or merging existing styles.

There are sudden bursts of energy with this placement, usually demonstrated verbally by the Mars in Aquarius saying something unexpected. This placement, like the other air Mars placements, is stimulated by socializing. However, Mars in Aquarius has a very impersonal way of moving forward through society. They are attracted more by ideas than they are to the people with the ideas. In a what would seem a strange way they seem to be attracted to indifference.

What this means for Mars in Aquarius:
Social causes and group social interaction inspire them. They have an interest in electronics, science, and art. Similarly to Mars in Gemini and Mars in Libra, they need some intellectual stimulation to accomplish physical tasks. This socialization is the external stimulation they need to get going.

> Mars in Aquarius Motivations: Ideas and social concepts. Indifference actually attracts. Science and electronics fields.

Famous mars in Aquarius people: Michelle Obama, Justin Bieber, Emma Watson, Alicia Keys, Gerard Butler, Jay-z, Tupac Shakur, Jada Pinkett Smith, Adrien Brody, Maya Angelou, Tony Robbins, Floyd Mayweather Jr.

Mars in Pisces

Mars in Pisces (mutable water) is a bit of a confusing place for Mars to occupy. Pisces deals with the supra 3D realm (i.e. the spirit world). Mars is action oriented and Pisces deals in the world of dreams and dissolution of the individual into the whole. So Mars in Pisces is not particularly self-motivated or assertive. However, they will put tireless energy into a spiritual ideal or idealistic cause. Anything relating to helping the sick, the incarcerated, the very young or old, or animals are the types of causes that Mars in Pisces will fight for.

Mars in Pisces needs their sleep more so than many of the other signs to retain their health and strength. Their ideals may also translate into art. Acting, dancing, and music are outlets where Mars in Pisces can step out of themselves and pretend to be someone else, or create the sound and rhythm that allows them to step away from the messiness of their day-to-day life.

What this means for Mars in Pisces:
They like animals and want to help others who are in need. The mythical realm of possibilities they see in the form of dreams, music, and art inspire them to create their own. They should find an altruistic purpose to pursue and make sure to get plenty of sleep. They tend to take action towards goals that may be totally unrealistic. It's important for their highly idealistic goals to be rooted in reality with a practical plan.

> Mars in Pisces Motivations: Caring for the sick and afflicted. Caring for animals. Political causes. Inspired by music, and dreams..

Famous Mars in Pisces people: Lebron James, Tom Hanks, Ricky Martin, Heath Ledger, Bob Dylan, John Cena, Phil Collins, Denzel Washington, Cindy Crawford, Paris Hilton, Tina Turner, Elton John, LL Cool J, Ray Liotta.

Final Thoughts on Mars

Mars has many ways of manifesting, and, as an individual, it's vitally important to know exactly what you can and cannot do. For example, if Mars is in an air sign, a solitary job that requires hard physical labor is not really going to work for you. A career that's more social and mentally-oriented would suit you better.

-6-
Faith (Jupiter)

The 6th and first "outer" or transpersonal planet in astrology is Jupiter. What we mean when we say transpersonal in astrology is that each "season" or sign for these planets has a very drawn out impact. Transpersonal planets are more about the era, than the individual person. However, each person is still impacted by these planets, some much more than others.

Jupiter is the planet of luck and faith. It describes what you have faith in and what will likely bring you good fortune. It amplifies whatever it touches (I will go into in more detail about this in the next book where we construct a *natal chart*). Jupiter also indicates wisdom and what areas an individual may have wisdom in. Jupiter is the great benefactor, the guardian angel. Every 12 years, Jupiter makes a full orbit and spends roughly one year in each sign. Due to its enormous size and as the largest planet in the solar system, Jupiter is king of the gods in astro-theology.

Jupiter is the sign of a woman's dream man

This is the man that a woman dreams about. These characteristics show her perfect and ideal husband.

Jupiter in Aries

Jupiter in Aries indicates that someone has faith and belief in their own abilities and also the abilities of others. This energy is a childlike energy, so they could have a blind faith approach to new situations. They usually lack perspective in their beliefs, leading to interpersonal quarrels based on a lack of understanding.

> ➤ Aptitudes and/or Benefits: Faith in self, instilling self-motivation and inner strength in others.

Famous Jupiter in Aries people: Brad Pitt, Russell Crowe, Whitney Houston, Robin Williams, Russell Brand, Tiger Woods, Sarah Palin, Zac Efron, Angelina Jolie, Lionel Messi, 50 Cent, Steven Seagal.

Jupiter in Taurus

Jupiter in Taurus shows wisdom with regards to accumulating wealth and possessions. They may be very generous and open with personal possessions and money. Taurus is a sensual sign, and Jupiter represents foreign cultures and languages. With Jupiter in Taurus, it is likely they are drawn to sensual pleasures that are not native to where they're from, for example foreign cuisine and foreign art. They also believe in faith manifesting itself in the tangible world, and are drawn to building monuments or houses of faith. Jupiter in Taurus is also prone to over-indulgence in sensual pleasure.

> ➤ Aptitudes and/or Benefits: Knowledge about making money, giving gifts. Attracts material possessions with less effort.

Famous Jupiter in Taurus people: Vladimir Putin, John Fitzgerald Kennedy, Sandra Bullock, Bruce Lee, Clive Owen, Floyd Mayweather Jr., Dr. Dre, Neil Diamond, Richard Pryor, Bob Dylan, Robert Downey Jr.

Jupiter in Gemini

Jupiter is in detriment here because Jupiter is ruled by Gemini's opposite, Sagittarius. This placement manifests as someone who is likely an inspirational speaker and skilled teacher. People who run into this individual may experience excessive chatter and gossip. Jupiter in Gemini typically likes to preach and may be seen as arrogant and self-righteous.

> ➤ <u>Aptitudes and/or Benefits</u>: Teaching, elementary education. Gains through speaking, and writing mediums.

Famous Jupiter in Gemini people: J.K. Rowling, Muhammed Ali, Charlie Sheen, Chris Brown, Kanye West, Oprah Winfrey, Howard Stern, Michael Moore, Tom Brady, Ben Stiller, Kim Bassinger.

Jupiter in Cancer

Jupiter is exalted in Cancer. The benevolent caretaking disposition of Cancer enjoys providing comfort to others. They are likely very open and generous with food and also open with their home. This person is more likely to have a large residence than sacrifice space to be in a large city environment. They naturally know how to "mother" other people. Jupiter in Cancer also indicates someone who receives benefits from family, like inheritance of property.

> ➤ <u>Aptitudes and/or Benefits</u>: Inheritance of land. Benefits through the hospitality industries. Large home. Attracts good fortune.

Famous Jupiter in Cancer people: Steve Jobs, Taylor Swift, Halle Berry, Jennifer Lawrence, James Franco, Nelson Mandela, Sean Connery, Jimi Hendrix, Heath Ledger, Warren Buffett.

Jupiter in Leo

Jupiter in Leo shares a similar benevolent disposition as its preceding sign, Cancer. However, in Leo there is a lot of attention placed on the rewards and status this benevolence will bring, which is the negative side of Leo. Wisdom and expansion through creative mediums such as film and fashion are shared by this placement. There is also a pronounced need to express oneself.

> Aptitudes and/or Benefits: Attracts good fortune through self-expression. Large ego.

Famous Jupiter in Leo people: Pink, Mick Jagger, Keith Richards, Julio Iglesias, Celine Dion, R. Kelly, George Lucas, Jimmy Page, Will Ferrell, Diana Ross, Whoopi Goldberg, Toni Braxton, Andy Garcia.

Jupiter in Virgo

Jupiter in Virgo is in detriment. Jupiter wants to have faith and trust in the natural course of life, but Virgo is a critical sign that relies on facts and data. The wise teacher, Jupiter in Virgo, thus looks for faults and errors in their pupils' work as opposed to providing them with inspiration. They have the wisdom and ability to spot tiny flaws and missing details, expanded mental faculties and capabilities, and they are more discriminating and discerning about alliances and associations.

> Aptitudes and/or Benefits: Healing others, fixing, organizing.

Famous Jupiter in Virgo people: Kim Kardashian, Bob Marley, Mel Gibson, Will Smith, Hugh Jackman, T.I., Joan Rivers, Anna Nicole Smith, Jamie Foxx, Tom Selleck, Helen Mirren.

Jupiter in Libra

Jupiter in Libra is the philosophical arbiter or lawyer. Libra likes to make judgements based in logic, but Jupiter in Libra will take morality into consideration as well. They exhibit wisdom of a political nature and can be well-versed in philosophies of law or the history of government. Jupiter in Libra individuals have a measured faith and can find luck through music and beauty.

> Aptitudes and/or Benefits: Diplomacy, making contractual deals, music, beauty.

Famous Jupiter in Libra people: Michael Jackson, Madonna, Jennifer Lopez, Jessica Alba, Miley Cyrus, Jay-Z, Adriana Lima, Bill Clinton, Jennifer Aniston, Prince, Justin Timberlake, Catherine Zeta-Jones .

Jupiter in Scorpio

Jupiter in Scorpio has wisdom in the field of investigation and research. They are an explorer of secrets and enjoy hidden and taboo subjects. They bear a deeply held faith that may not be shared. They could be someone who travels to or lives in foreign lands. They search for hidden truths and have knowledge of the occult arts and sciences. Jupiter in Scorpio has an intense need for intimacy.

> Aptitudes and/or Benefits: Exploring, researching the unknown. Benefits through inheritance.

Famous Jupiter in Scorpio people: Matt Damon, DMX, Jessica Biel, Mariah Carey, Nicki Minaj, Sade Adu, Deepak Chopra, Arnold Schwarzenegger, Justin Bieber, Lil Wayne, Hugh Laurie, Aleister Crowley.

Jupiter in Sagittarius

Jupiter is in domicile in Sagittarius, so strong belief systems are promoted. Higher education and religious/spiritual beliefs are internalized and expressed as well. A Jupiter in Sagittarius individual has a natural faith and trust that life events will take their course and work themselves out. They benefit from higher education and teaching and can be an inspirational and motivational teacher.

> ➤ Aptitudes and/or Benefits: Benefitting through the teaching of higher knowledge, especially related to religion and faith.

Famous Jupiter in Sagittarius people: Cameron Diaz, Hillary Clinton, Ben Affleck, Amy Winehouse, Kendall Jenner, Snoop Dogg, Eckhart Tolle, Amber Rose, Erykah Badu, Tony Robbins.

Jupiter in Capricorn

Jupiter in Capricorn is in fall. This is someone who has faith in establishments like government institutions and companies that they bring these spiritual benefits to the masses. They tend to believe that order and discipline will increase the value of an individual's life. A Jupiter in Capricorn's beliefs are rigid and don't transcend the physical world or pragmatism.

> ➤ Aptitudes and/or Benefits: Government work, managerial positions.

Famous Jupiter in Capricorn people: Eminem, Bono, Adolf Hitler, Prince Harry of Wales, Walt Disney, Pope Francis, Mark Zuckerberg, Jack Nicholson, Morgan Freeman, Sofia Vergara, Bruce Jenner.

Jupiter in Aquarius

Jupiter in Aquarius describes someone who has a belief in science and esoteric science. The burden of proof for them is high, however. They want to understand the steps and perspectives that make the particular science work. It must make logical sense to them. Concepts that benefit the masses of people are something they may believe in.

> ➤ Aptitudes and/or Benefits: Science, technological innovation. Faith in humanity.

Famous Jupiter in Aquarius people: Barack Obama, Jim Carrey, Tyra Banks, Heidi Klum, Eddie Murphy, Ciara, Eva Mendes, Paul Walker, Joseph Stalin, Kylie Jenner, Jeff Bridges, Bill Murray.

Jupiter in Pisces

Jupiter in Pisces is exalted. Knowledge flows directly to them from a divine intuition. This is the spiritualist, and they believe in practices like meditation and solitude. Care for the poor and the sick brings these people good will.

> ➢ Aptitudes and/or Benefits: Spirituality and higher consciousness. Benefitting through caretaking of the underprivileged, sick, and afflicted.

Famous Jupiter in Pisces people: Lady Gaga, Tina Turner, Drake, Victoria Beckham, Jon Stewart, Emmy Rossum, Steve Carell, Marvin Gaye, Nelly, Wesley Snipes, Sidney Poitier.

Final Thoughts on Jupiter

Jupiter expands and inflates whatever sign it touches. When you look up your own Jupiter, think about what approach you've had to religion in life. What is your attitude towards risk or leaps of faith? How does your Jupiter work with or against your other planets?

-7-

Structure (Saturn)

In astrology, the final planet that has one of the 12 signs as a ruler is Saturn. Saturn is at home in Capricorn, exalted in Libra and debilitated in Aries, Leo, and Cancer. Saturn works in the opposite way of Jupiter. Where Jupiter expands, Saturn restricts. Saturn shows where a person needs to improve (qualities that don't come to them easily) and the process needed to achieve that improvement. Saturn is a slow moving planet, and, as such, it takes 30 and a ½ years to complete its cycle. Saturn is known as the taskmaster, requiring each of us to work through certain personal issues to become an adult and a "complete" person.

Saturn in Aries

Saturn in Aries is in fall because Saturn requires patience, and Aries is a sign of swift action. These individuals are likely to work very hard for what they want; however, they tend to have the "I'm an island of a person" attitude. They will forge ahead without help. They enjoy working and will work hard even after their defined goals have been reached.

> Areas to Work on: Self-actualization, self-confidence.

Famous Saturn in Aries people: Jennifer Aniston, Pamela Anderson, Will Smith, Celine Dion, Tina Turner, Jason Statham, Vin Diesel, Chuck Norris, Morgan Freeman, Owen Wilson, Renee Zellweger.

Saturn in Taurus

Saturn in Taurus wants to accumulate possessions and wealth. Saturn delays both of these things in favor of pushing the individual to save and build over the long term. This person probably has an IRA and is slowly accumulating a nest egg for later on in life. They may be seen as frugal or "cheap".

> ➤ Areas to Work on: Respect for the value of earned money and possessions.

Famous Saturn in Taurus people: Jay-Z, Jennifer Lopez, Mariah Carey, Bruce Lee, Mark Wahlberg, Naomi Campbell, Al Pacino, Puff Daddy, Queen Latifah, Jack Black, Kely Ripa, DMX, Dick Cheney, John Gotti.

Saturn in Gemini

Saturn in Gemini is the individual who probably was a poor communicator early on in life. They may struggle with communication in their early school years, but through work and practice they can become a competent communicator, whether it be written, vocal, or musical.

> ➤ Areas to Work on: Communication. Speaking and writing specifically. Understanding human interaction.

Famous Saturn in Gemini people: Eminem, Alyssa Milano, Jimi Hendrix, Jimmy Page, Billie Holiday, George Harrison, Snoop Dogg, Dwayne Johnson, James Blunt, Martin Scorsese.

Saturn in Cancer

Saturn in Cancer is in Saturn's detriment. Saturn in Cancer is someone who had a very serious mother. This person had their emotions withheld while growing up, and, because of that early behavior, they will likely have trouble connecting on an emotional level with others. That intimacy that Cancer craves is met with fear of betrayal by Saturn.

> Areas to Work on: Empathy, intimacy, self-nurturing.

Famous Saturn in Cancer people: Leonardo DiCaprio, Bob Marley, Colin Ferrell, George W. Bush, Jimmy Fallon, Kirk Douglas, Nas, Seth McFarlane, Nelly, Jewel, Derek Jeter.

Saturn in Leo

Saturn in Leo is in fall. This placement indicates a fear of the big stage, and a general disapproval of performing arts and creativity. This is mostly due to fear of disappointment, especially disappointing the father. This fear of the big stage is worked on by doing something that requires them to perform in front of others. Over time, this fear is conquered.

> Areas to Work on: Creative courage, self-expression, self-confidence.

Famous Saturn in Leo people: Hillary Clinton, Bill Clinton, Mitt Romney, Kanye West, Elton John, John Mayer, Tom Brady, Tiger Woods, Floyd Mayweather Jr., Tom Hardy.

Saturn in Virgo

Saturn in Virgo is the pessimist. This indicates someone who looks for their environment to be in perfect order. Small details that don't bother many people will bother them. This stems from constantly being criticized or held to a standard they couldn't meet while growing up. So creating perfection and order is something they work on throughout their life and master in their later years.

➢ Areas to Work on: Organization, refraining from hypercriticism of self and others.

Famous Saturn in Virgo people: Robin Williams, Stevie Wonder, Richard Gere, Michelle Williams, Richard Branson, Bruce Springsteen, Bruce Jenner, Bruce Jenner, Kobe Bryant.

Saturn in Libra

Saturn in Libra is exalted. The thrifty and workaholic nature of Saturn is met here by square dealing Libra. Saturn isn't afraid to work hard and get their hands dirty and Libra wants to make deals and make them fair. This also indicates fair marriages, a marriage where things are equitable in the union as well as in the divorce.

➢ Areas to Work on: Creating and maintaining relationships, being diplomatic, working with others.

Famous Saturn in Libra people: Beyonce Knowles, Jessica Alba, Alicia Keys, Tony Blair, George H.W. Bush, Mila Kunis, Tony Parker, Nick Cannon, Ed Harris, Meagan Good, Keyshia Cole.

Saturn in Scorpio

Saturn in Scorpio shows someone who fears change. Scorpio is a transformative sign and Saturn's reluctance to take risks shows that they have an intense attachment to keep things the way they are. However, if they latch onto something they want, they will work with feverish intensity and shut out all other things. Underhanded tactics may be used too because, as a Mars sign, the goal is to win.

➢ Areas to Work on: Accepting change as it comes, becoming flexible. Becoming comfortable with intimacy.

Famous Saturn in Scorpio people: Nicki Minaj, Mark Zuckerberg, Kevin Costner, Linda Goodman, Steve Jobs, Oprah Winfrey, Bill Gates, Tom Hanks, Bruce Willis, Ciara, Lebron James.

Saturn in Sagittarius

Saturn in Sagittarius shows a person who believes in a philosophy that can be readily applied in the real world. This person wants tangible results for their philosophy, too, but this also indicates delays and a kind of rigidity. Where Jupiter in Sagittarius wants to explore different schools of thought, Saturn in Sagittarius finds one and may stick with it for a very long time, possibly even for life. This is the religious leader, for example, who leads a service in the same religious institution in the same way for many years.

> ➢ Areas to Work on: Higher education, becoming comfortable with traveling and understanding foreign cultures.

Famous Saturn in Sagittarius people: Megan Fox, Grace Kelly, Martin Luther King Jr., Madonna, Michael Jackson, Lady Gaga, Prince, Zac Efron, Ellen DeGeneres, Sharon Stone, Usain Bolt.

Saturn in Capricorn

Saturn in Capricorn is one of its domicile placements. This indicates someone who will organize and work hard to achieve status in the world. This person doesn't mind hard work and has patience and the perseverance to see an objective through to the end. They appreciate order, or at least their own specific order of getting things done.

> ➢ Areas to Work on: Career progression, attaining status.

Famous Saturn in Capricorn people: Barack Obama, George Clooney,

Taylor Swift, Chris Brown, Jennifer Lawrence, Bono, Eddie Murphy, Tony Robbins, Ray Charles, Rita Ora, Kevin Spacey.

Saturn in Aquarius

Saturn is also in domicile in Aquarius. Saturn here is capable of organizing and understanding the mechanics of large entities. This includes large social organizations, businesses, and so on. This placement reveals someone who works for and amongst the masses, ranging from the lowest rung on the ladder all the way to the top. Saturn in Aquarius tries to look at all the parts of a large system objectively.

> ➤ <u>Areas to Work on</u>: Objective analysis, impartiality. Working with all types of humans regardless of race, ethnicity, religion, sexual orientation, and so on.

Famous Saturn in Aquarius people: Brad Pitt, Michelle Obama, Tom Cruise, Jim Carrey, Michael Jordan, Aleister Crowley, Johnny Cash, Sarah Palin, Jon Stewart, James Brown, Jet Li.

Saturn in Pisces

Saturn wants to remain grounded at all times, so Saturn in Pisces is a placement that shows someone who has a tough time connecting with the imagination and with the arts, like poetry and music. Saturn in Pisces has to work very hard when mastering an art form such as photography or music. This may also manifest as someone who ends up working very hard on understanding higher spirituality and empathy.

> ➤ <u>Areas to Work on</u>: Spiritual receptivity, openness.

Famous Saturn in Pisces People: Kurt Cobain, Justin Bieber, Halle Berry,

Robert Downey Jr., Janet Jackson, Lenny Kravitz, Adam Sandler, Ben Stiller, John McCain, R.Kelly, Steven Colbert, Burt Reynolds.

Final Thoughts on Saturn

These placements sum up the different fears individuals suffer from and what they might struggle with. In order to get beyond such fears and struggles, an individual must work through these issues and that's what Saturn forces us to do.

-8-

The Retrograde

Retrograde is a term in astronomy and astrology that means a planet in orbit appears to be moving backwards. In actuality, it is just slowing down. In astrology, retrograde periods indicate that planets will express themselves differently. In astrological software or reading materials, you can identify the retrograde planets by an *Rx* after a particular planet's symbol. The retrograde planet means different things for different planets. For example, Mars Rx is not very beneficial. In Saturn, though, it can be very beneficial.

Mercury retrograde

This placement is known as a troublemaker. You may hear it referenced in movies and television for its effects on communications and travel. If you were born under a Mercury retrograde it just means that your thought process operates more carefully. "Slower on the uptake" could probably be applied here. In order to deal with their latent thought process, these people tend to have a rich inner world of communication and creativity that is not verbalized.

Venus retrograde

Venus is the expression of love and sociability and when Venus is in retrograde this is channeled inward or expressed much differently. They probably have hobbies related to Venus (art, fashion, music) that they do alone and don't share with many people. This can be a social hindrance and prevent someone from making contacts, so it is important to be conscious of it and attempt to appropriately modify that behavior.

Mars retrograde

Mars Rx sends Mars inward leading to the individual channeling Mars in a way that creates an urge to work quietly and express anger in a different manner. This might lead to self-destructive behavior if not properly channeled.

Jupiter retrograde

Jupiter RX puts people into a position where they question their faith and belief systems continuously. This person finds a spiritual system or religion that they believe in then find something else that they identify with and end up unsure which one works for them. This is also someone who, when they have bad luck, doesn't learn why and it takes them a long time to understand the causes of things.

Saturn retrograde

Saturn in retrograde works to Saturn's benefit because it unlocks Saturn. Saturn by nature is solitary, so, in retrograde, Saturn becomes something that works openly and outwardly. This creates opportunities to be more assertive in getting things done and get them done faster.

Uranus in retrograde

Uranus in retrograde is a time of extreme and abrupt changes en masse. Changes in government due to a shift in public ideology and philosophy are likely.

Neptune in Retrograde

Neptune in retrograde shows a period where lies and deceit are revealed. The veil is lifted and people, places, and things previously under false identities are exposed. Hidden communications are also revealed.

Pluto in retrograde

Pluto in retrograde will destroy what is established but does not work for the public at large. Humanity is forced to make choices, many of which are very difficult choices like whether or not a nation should go to war.

-9-

Destiny (Your North Node)

There is a lunar pole in astrology that shows what kind of destiny you are headed towards called the North Node of the Moon or True Node sign. This counters the South Node of the Moon which shows the qualities we have already mastered. Your North Node sign may or may not have compatibility with the rest of the chart which might make reaching this North Node point more difficult. If your Sun Sign is in the same or a compatible sign of your North Node, this progress becomes much easier and more straightforward.

If you do some research and ask your friends and acquaintances what their sign is, you will likely find many of them are your North Node sign. This can be true even if they don't really seem compatible with your Sun Sign or other natal chart placements. Some consider this sign equally as important as the Sun Sign or Moon Sign.

Your North Node in Aries

This shows a need to learn independence, courage, and other Aries traits. These people must learn to take action and to trust their own judgement. They should cultivate self-reliance and self-concern and not give into the wishes of others for the sake of peace and not making waves.

North Node in Taurus

A person with this North Node placement should come down into their body. In other words, they should become comfortable with the material world and the 5 senses. They must cultivate a practical attitude in order to tackle problems and following realistic steps to achieve goals. It is important for them to create healthy boundaries and become self-reliant.

North Node in Gemini

Someone with their North Node in Gemini needs to become a better logical thinker and approach issues that need to be tackled with more tact and care. Listening skills must be developed. Fact checking and jumping to conclusions needs to be abandoned. For this person, self-righteousness and making assumptions are cautioned against.

North Node in Cancer

North Node in Cancer shows a person who has to cultivate more empathy. They need to learn to accept others' feelings while accepting their own feelings. North Node in Cancer wants us to come home so to speak, so they should build up their own home base and family structure for security. It is important they share their feelings and fears with their relationship partner and let go of needing to be the "boss" in every situation.

North Node in Leo

People with their North Node in Leo need to develop their childlike creativity and their willingness to courageously follow their heart. By standing up for themselves and being their own person, they will find their way. They should get their heart in the game and try to avoid the crutch of aloofness when a situation requires action.

North Node in Virgo

With this placement, it is important to engage in the physical world, to participate as opposed to daydream. Refining one's plans and organizing is vital. They need to be grounded and do the proper preparation and planning for upcoming events, big or small. They also should make sound and concrete decisions and stick by them. This will make all the difference in the world.

North Node in Libra

North Node in Libra people must develop the skills of tact and collaboration. Sharing must be developed and they should resist selfishness. Childish rushes into action, impulsiveness, and poor judgement should be attributes they try to modify.

North Node in Scorpio

For North Node in Scorpio individuals, building inner strength and letting go of possessions that serve no purpose are what will keep them on the right track. This person should work on developing discipline. Any habits that cause stagnation in their personal progress should be changed, and they should let go of their resistance to change.

North Node in Sagittarius

North Node in Sagittarius is considered to be in fall. Sagittarius represents knowledge, and Gemini represents the communication of knowledge. So they should learn how to communicate before they acquire knowledge. They also need to learn to trust their heart and intuition. Finally, they would do well to abandon their tendency to gossip.

North Node in Capricorn

This individual must learn the virtues of persistence and self-control. They should let go of the past and allow themselves to take calculated risks. It is recommended they use a practical approach to solve problems and not allow emotional breakdowns to stop them from doing so.

North Node in Aquarius

North Node in Aquarius people must embrace objectivity and abandon the need to have their own way all of the time. They need to humble themselves and make friends by associating with all types of people regardless of status or background. Abandoning their need for approval and their need to impress others is also important.

North Node in Pisces

North Node in Pisces people need to learn compassion and empathy. These individuals tend to be highly critical and anxious. It is important for them to develop a spiritual connection with life and try to mitigate the need to be perfect and always in control.

Final Thoughts on the North Node

These 12 different paths are extremely important. Unfortunately, for some reason, many astrologers do not put enough emphasis on these aspects of the *natal chart*. They are important, though, because they give hints about what activities are worthwhile. As I said earlier, if a person is born with a certain North Node they tend to constantly run into a specific sign. Learn everything you can about that particular North Node, and how people of that sign conduct themselves. These are qualities that should be applied to the North Node person's life to help in their own fulfillment.

-10-
Conclusion

The 7 celestial bodies and the North Node make up most of the puzzle pieces needed to analyze ourselves astrologically. These pieces can be combined to paint a good portion of the total picture of a person. To give you an example, say a person is born on April 28th, and, at the time of their birth, the Moon was in Gemini. That would make them an individual with a Taurus Sun and a Gemini Moon. Referring back to the first 2 chapters we can see that those individual placements are quite different. On one side there is the soul of an earthy Taurus, who is interested in practicality and interacting with the world in a tactile way. But the Moon is in airy Gemini, so this person could actually be more comfortable and at ease in their head, and very content with being a curious and inquisitive person; however, In order for their soul to be content, they would have to engage their senses and build something concrete in the world.

Earth and Air elements do not work together. so this person will have to find some type of career or relationship situation that plays to both of those needs. They might, for example, be very different people in the public and the private setting. With this combination, there will likely always be some pull away from one placement's needs. It will be very uncomfortable for this Taurus to handle mundane practical tasks while their Gemini Moon mind is running 100 miles per minute. The Gemini Moon will need to cultivate some willpower and pragmatism to accomplish what the Taurus Sun placement requires.

This complex relationship between the Sun and the Moon can be applied to the other planets as well. This is how the planets create a unique collage for every single person on earth. The ascendant sign, which is based on a person's time and place of birth, is also an important aspect one should be aware of. However, the ascendant sign has been left out of this book because, to comprehend that completely, we need to understand a full chart. Likewise, the modern outer planets of Uranus, Neptune, and Pluto are also missing. They will be explained in the next book. Once these planets are placed in a natal chart, complete with an ascendant sign and modern planets, along with the geometry (or aspect) of the planets for each particular birthdate, a complex collage is created that reveals a unique cosmic self-portrait. This self- portrait can be used to understand and guide an individual as long as they live.

-11-
Tables and Definitions

The previous 10 chapters gave a foundation for understanding the different pieces of a particular natal chart; however, an individual's natal chart is complex and nuanced. The tables and definitions below provide a resource for further decoding and understanding the natal chart.

Spring
♈ Aries- Cardinal-Fire
♉ Taurus-Fixed-Earth
♊ Gemini-Mutable-Air

Summer
♋ Cancer-Cardinal-Water
♌ Leo-Fixed-Fire
♍ Virgo-Mutable-Earth

Fall
♎ Libra-Cardinal-Air
♏ Scorpio-Fixed-Water
♐ Sagittarius-Mutable-Fire

Winter
♑ Capricorn-Cardinal-Earth
♒ Aquarius-Fixed-Air
♓ Pisces-Mutable-Water

Planetary Symbols

SUN

MOON

MERCURY

VENUS

MARS

JUPITER

SATURN

URANUS

NEPTUNE

PLUTO

CHIRON

LUNAR NODE

LILITH

Element legend

Elements

4   1

3   2

■ 1-Air-Logic   ■ 2-Fire-Passion
■ 3-Earth-Pragmatism ■ 4-Water-Emotion

In most books and natal chart software readouts, the sign elements will correspond with the colors in the above legend.

Modalities of the signs

Modalities

3   1
     2

⁄ 1-Cardinal- Initiation, assertiveness
Ⅱ 2-Fixed- Maintainence, stablity
3-Mutable-Versatility, communication

Above, the lines indicate the rhythm of the different sign modalities. The red diagonal lines show the Cardinal modality (Aries, Cancer, Libra,

Capricorn). This modality is forward moving. The green vertical lines represent the fixed signs (Taurus, Leo, Scorpio, Aquarius). These individuals work towards control and consistency. Lastly, the blue squares in section #3 represent the mutable signs (Gemini, Virgo, Sagittarius, Pisces). These signs represent versatility.

Classical Temperaments

In classical astrology, the theory of "temperaments" originated in the idea that the elements of astrology are fluid and combine to create various admixtures. These temperaments describe a person's demeanor.

Wet: (Air, Water elements)—Making connections. Water energy makes connections emotionally and intimately. Air makes these connections intellectually and socially. Air represents humanity and refinement.

Dry: (Fire, Earth elements)—Self-motivated. Earth is a worker focused on practical tasks. Fire is focused on action, and courage. Both of which do not take others into the decision making process.

Hot: (Fire, Air)—Extraversion

Cold: (Earth, Water)—Introversion

Choleric: Aggression, energy, assertiveness. Makes decisions based on intuition. (Aries, Leo, Sagittarius)

Sanguine: Friendliness, sociability, intellectualism. Makes decisions based in logic. (Gemini, Libra, Aquarius)

Melancholic: Self-sufficient, lacking cheerfulness, worldly ambitious. Relies on data and statistics in their calculation process. (Taurus, Virgo, Capricorn)

Phlegmatic: Emotional, indolent, receptive. They rely on their feelings in the calculation process. (Cancer, Scorpio, Pisces)

Sign and planet power table

	Domicile	Exalted	Fall	Detriment
Sun	Leo	Aries	Libra	Aquarius
Moon	Cancer	Taurus	Scorpio	Capricorn
Mercury	Gemini and Virgo			Sagittarius and Pisces
Venus	Libra and Taurus	Pisces	Virgo	Aries and Scorpio
Mars	Aries and Scorpio	Capricorn	Cancer	Libra and Taurus
Jupiter	Sagittarius and Pisces	Cancer	Capricorn	Gemini and Virgo
Saturn	Capricorn and Aquarius	Libra	Aries	Cancer and Leo

Table 1 Domicile = Full Power, Detriment lowest power

-12-
Tools

To learn the planets and signs of an individual, there is natal chart software available. For the adventurous, an ephemeris[16] can also be used. The most efficient way, though is to use a natal chart generator. Below is a list of resources:

Natal Chart Generators

Vocation natal chart generator for Windows: Vocation Natal Chart Generator or http://astro-chologist.com/Vocation_v110_install.exe

Aquarius2go astrology app for Android: Aquarius2go astrology or https://play.google.com/store/apps/details?id=net.wilfinger.aquarius2go&hl=en

Natal Charts for IOS : Natal Charts or https://itunes.apple.com/us/app/natal-charts/id325367776?mt=8

Free online generator : http://alabe.com/freechart/

---

[16] Data bank of planet and sign movements.

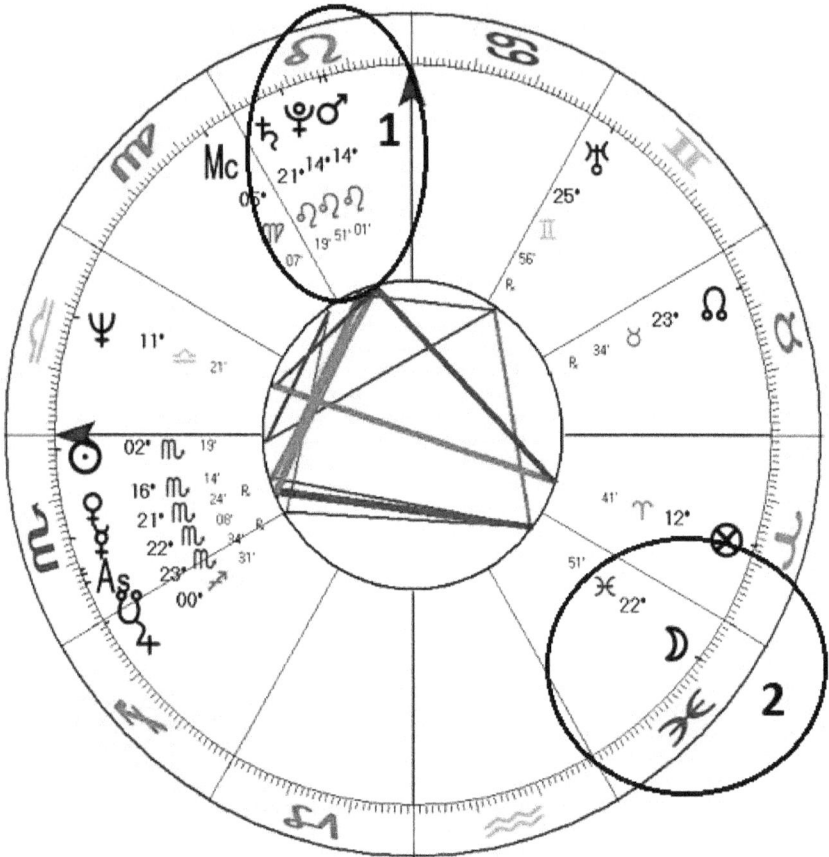

Table 2

Locating the planets and signs in the chart

Once a person's information is added into the natal chart generator, a chart that looks like the one pictured in table 2 will appear. Take a closer look at the chart to identify each of the signs.

In figure 1, I've identified the sign of Leo which is in the outer ring of the chart. Right below the Leo symbol is the symbol for Mars. Below that, it says "14" with a degree symbol. That indicates that Mars is "in Leo", at 14 degrees. Each sign comprises 30 degrees (12 x 30 = 360 degrees).

In figure 2 the sign of Pisces appears in the outer ring. Above it is the symbol for the Moon. Slightly above that symbol, the number "22" appears. This indicates that their Moon is in Pisces at 22 degrees.

This person has their Moon in Pisces, and Mars in Leo, so they can refer to those sections in the book to learn more about their temperament.

Lastly, the "horseshoe" shape in the chart right in between Scorpio and Sagittarius shows the North Node.

Want a reading? Contact me
http://astro-chologist.com/contact/

Have an Astrology Question?
Ask @ Ask a question
http://astro-chologist.com/ask-question/questions/

Follow me on Twitter @ Astrochologist
https://twitter.com/Astrochologist

Follow Me on Facebook @ Astrochologist Fanpage
https://www.facebook.com/Astrochologist

About the author

Seth Morris is a writer, author, and political scientist from New Jersey. He has a degree in political science and has been a practicing professional astrologer for nearly 10 years. He's a writer and the owner of astro-chologist.com which explores facets of practical and conceptual Astrology that tend to be untouched. As a political scientist, he has worked for local campaigns in the state of New Jersey. He enjoys sports, and playing the guitar and bass in his leisure time.

Notes

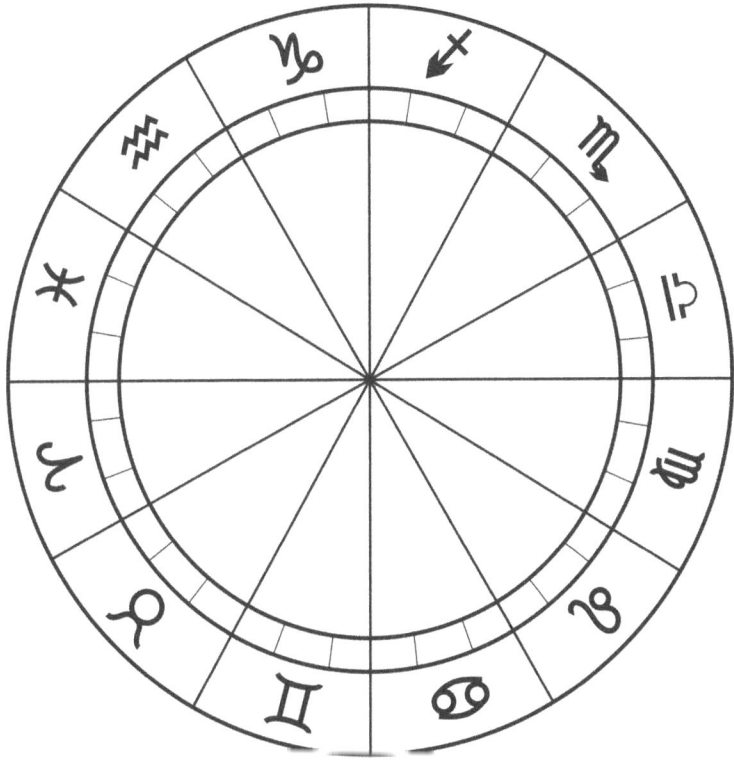

_____ 's Natal Chart

Sun in_____

Moon in _____

Mercury in _____

Venus in _____

Mars in_____

Jupiter in_____

Saturn in_____

References

Astrology: Advanced Search, Multicriteria. (n.d.). Retrieved May 14, 2015, from http://www.astrotheme.com/celebrities/search_by_astrological_criteria.php

Babies' biological clocks dramatically affected by birth light cycle. (2010, December 6). Retrieved May 8, 2015, from http://news.vanderbilt.edu/2010/12/babies-biological-clocks-dramatically-affected-by-birth-light-cycle/

Bucheli, P. (n.d.). Retrieved June 2, 2015, from http://www.ncbi.nlm.nih.gov/books/NBK92756/

Burk, K. (2001). *Astrology: Understanding the birth chart : A comprehensive guide to classical interpretation.* St. Paul, Minn.: Llewellyn Publications.

Frawley, J. (2001). *The real astrology.* London. Apprentice.

George, L., & Bytheriver, M. (1986). *The new A to Z horoscope maker and delineator* (13th ed.). St. Paul, Minn., U.S.A.: Llewellyn Publications.

Gibson, M. (1998). *Signs of mental illness.* St. Paul, MN: Llewellyn Publications.

Lycopene, Tomatoes, and the Prevention of Coronary Heart Disease. (n.d.). Retrieved April 7, 2015, from http://ebm.sagepub.com/content/227/10/908.abstract

Robbins, F. (1980). *Tetrabiblos.* Cambridge, Mass.: Harvard University Press ;.

Spiller, J. (2008). *Astrology for the soul.* New York: Bantam Books.

Coming Soon…

The Road from space : how to *manifest* in the 21st century